"Ron Susek's newest book is a compelling story of faith and courage. It stands in the tradition of the great missionary biographies of all time. Read it for yourself and give it to a friend. You will both be blessed."

—Dr. Jerry Falwell, Chancellor
Liberty University, Lynchburg, VA

"This is a story that should stir young and old to aspire to greater heights of dedication to Christ and service for God and His kingdom. Ernst and Sigrid Vatter were missionaries of the highest Christian caliber. They faced every conceivable trial and testing in their work, but triumphed graciously. The unspeakable tragedies and terrors that surrounded September 11, 2001, brought forth incredible stories of bravery and victory of men and women in the natural world and we honor them; but here, in this missionary classic, is the record of similar heroism and optimism in the spiritual world that calls for similar recognition and emulation. Read this book and you will never be the same again. You will want to serve your Lord—holding nothing back."

—Dr. Stephen F. Olford, Chairman and Founder
The Center for Biblical Preaching

"One of the greatest blessings that can come to the contemporary church is to hear the story of great missionaries of our Lord, whose stories often are not known here in the North American continent. Ron Susek has provided in this biographical treatment of a marvelous German missionary, Dr. Ernst Vatter, a riveting biography with a profoundly hopeful spiritual message for our day. This will bless your soul."

—Dr. Paige Patterson, President
Southeastern Baptist Theological Seminary
Wake Forest, NC

"The life of Ernst Vatter is the consummate twentieth-century story of God's grace. With skill and clarity, Ron Susek unwraps this fascinating life in Holding Nothing Back, taking us into the world of post-Nazi Germany, through the challenges of missionary life in Japan and behind the scenes of the remarkable expansion of the Liebenzell Mission. Told in a charming and captivating way, this is a story of tragedy and triumph, life and love, courage and commitment that you will want to read again and again."

—Woodrow Kroll, President
Back to the Bible International

"Holding Nothing Back chronicles Dr. Ernst Vatter's simple yet profound dedication to die to self and live in obedience to our great God and Savior. This account will inspire every believer."

—Dr. Bill Bright, Founder
Campus Crusade for Christ

"To learn about Ernst Vatter's life-long journey, through the excellent penmanship of Ron Susek, is an unforgettable experience. Susek is a master storyteller. His uncanny skill of selecting the most fitting and effective words at the right time and in the right place, creates a heart-moving mood. The readers will feel transported from situation to situation, on the one hand identifying with the main characters of the story, and on the other hand deeply touched by their actions."

—Dr. Reinhold K. Kerstan, Professor Emeritus
Preaching and Communications
Sarasota, FL

"The life of Ernst Vatter is a pilgrimage. This gripping story of a man always on the edge of his faith and seeing God deliver in the most desperate situations will lift your spirit and encourage you to trust God in every circumstance."

—Dr. Jerry E. White, President
The Navigators

Holding Nothing Back

Ernst Vatter, A Portrait of Perseverance

Ron Susek

CHRISTIAN PUBLICATIONS, INC.
CAMP HILL, PENNSYLVANIA

CHRISTIAN PUBLICATIONS, INC.

3825 Hartzdale Drive, Camp Hill, PA 17011
www.christianpublications.com

Faithful, biblical publishing since 1883

Holding Nothing Back
0-87509-968-8
© 2002 by Ron Susek
All rights reserved
Printed in the United States of America

02 03 04 05 06   5 4 3 2 1

Contents

Is This the Warrior's End?

June 1999. Ernst Vatter lay flat on his back, unable to lift his seventy-year-old head from the pillow. In three days he was to depart for Palau, an island in the western Pacific, to speak at a conference for ministers. Over the past four decades he had experienced the assault of a debilitating weakness just prior to most of his numerous trips to speak in foreign nations. This time, however, it held a stronger grip than usual. *Is this the end?* he wondered.

"Sigrid," he said to his wife, "I think this time we need to call the doctor. I don't think I can make it. It has never been this bad before."

"No doctor!" she replied firmly. "We've been through this many times. The doctors never find a thing. We know what it is: The devil wants to stop you."

"I know that's true, but this time it feels different. I'm so weak. I don't have enough strength to raise my head."

Ernst didn't want to speak of dying, although he sensed its hooded presence. The reality of death was not new to him. He had lived one short stride ahead of it for years, ever since it first approached him as a young husband and father. The damage to his body back then had left doctors scratching their heads about what kept him alive. Avoiding the word "miracle" they called it "a phenomenon," refusing to mix God with medical science. One doctor even wanted to do exploratory surgery to search for the reason. "Nonsense," Ernst replied. "I don't need to be cut open for the answer. I'll accept my life as a gift from the Lord and leave it at that."

Now, many years later, it felt as though death had finally caught its long-sought prey. "Perhaps you should call my contact in Palau and tell him that I can't come," Ernst said to Sigrid, his voice frail. "How can I go and preach when I can't even lift my head?"

"No, I will not call anyone in Palau, and I will not call the doctor," Sigrid said as she knelt beside him. She folded her hands and prayed aloud: "Dear heavenly Father, my husband and I have committed ourselves to serve You. Your Son said that without Him we can do nothing. We know that to be true. Now we need You to break this attack upon Ernst and strengthen him by Your mighty right hand, enabling him to preach in Palau."

When she had finished, nothing changed. It was just her and Ernst alone in a quiet room. Undaunted, she rose from her knees, patted her husband on the arm and said, "You'll be all right. The Lord will strengthen you. You will go to Palau."

She doesn't understand, Ernst said to himself. *This time I may not make it. The weakness is too great. I'm not sure I'll even survive.* Sigrid's confidence, however, cast a thin shaft of hope through the window of his heart. Deep inside he knew she was right.

Over the following days, he had no choice but to surrender to the weakness and hope in God. It became a time of reflection, a time to relive the life he had known. He thought of the time many years earlier when he had made a choice to wholeheartedly serve God, clinging to the promise in Psalm 84:11, "No good thing does he withhold from those whose walk is blameless."

He had proven that to be true many times over, knowing that apart from God's strength enabling him to persevere, he would not be alive. Yet even as he reflected on what God had done for him in the past, a voice deep within cried out to prove God's unwavering faithfulness in his latter years as well. He felt that his life's work wasn't finished yet, but now his strength was rapidly diminishing.

His thoughts wandered back to his childhood and the strange way his life of ministry had begun.

CHAPTER ONE

The Boy and His Pillow

Ernst stood frozen against the kitchen doorjamb. Huge tears rimmed his eyes, revealing his fear—fear that his world was crumbling and there was nothing he could do to hold it together. He needed security, but the atmosphere volcanically spewed threat. His two older brothers and sister huddled in the living room. Two baby brothers were upstairs in their beds.

Neighbors in the small southwest village of Goenningen, Germany, cringed: Ernst Vatter's father, Victor, was drunk again. His mother, Ernstine, pleaded, "Victor, you need to do something about your drinking—maybe go to church."

"Why should I go to church?" Victor roared, his eyes puffed and glassy. Words slurred across his alcohol-thickened tongue. "I can be a hypocrite and talk about other people without going to church."

"Please don't say such things so loudly, Victor. This is a small village, and everyone already knows you drink too much."

"Don't you dare say I drink too much, woman. I'll do whatever I want! Nobody can tell me what to do."

"Please, stop. The children can hear you. Ernst is only two, but he understands what you're saying."

"The kids! That's all you think about. Leave me alone!" he growled.

Ernstine's fingers quivered as she retied her apron. She enfolded Ernst in her arms, and he cried openly. Victor clopped out of the kitchen, flopped into bed and fell into a deep sleep, snoring loudly. Sunrise generally found his gregarious personality restored, but everyone knew that the next drink would reawaken the raging bull.

* * *

Hours later sun rays broke over the Alb Mountain Range and poured through chalet windows. Roosters pierced the silence, officially announcing dawn. Several work horses that Victor kept stomped and snorted in the stables under the house. Little Ernst awakened to his mother's soft voice singing. Her buoyant heart warmed their home, filling it with hope. But this was not to be just another day. The boy would shock everyone with an act that not only revealed his nature, but altered his future as well.

Ernst, who had been born on March 18, 1929, was the fourth of six children. His parents were members of the Lutheran Church located just a stone's throw down the hill from their small home. It had a large steeple pointing heavenward, a direction few villagers ever looked except when disaster struck. Ernst's parents neither attended the church, nor had they experienced the life-changing rebirth discovered by Martin Luther during the Great Reformation—a rebirth that came when he threw off the idea of salvation by works.

"Ernstine? . . . Ernstine? . . ." called a woman's voice.

"Oh, good morning, Sofie." It was Victor's sister, who was married to Ernst Hermann. "What a beautiful spring morning. Come, sit down. I'll get you some coffee."

Generally cheery, this day Sofie lowered her head and dabbed tears from her eyes. "You can't imagine, Ernstine, how hard it is not to have children . . . and you have six. Is it not possible for one of them to come and live with me?"

Ernstine felt compassion mingle with frustration. How could she give up one of her children? They were her very breath. Ernst clutched his aunt's dress, his big eyes looking into her face. She was one of his favorite relatives.

"Good morning, Sofie!" Victor bellowed as he swung around the corner and entered the kitchen. "Get me some coffee and breakfast," he ordered Ernstine. At least he was in a better temperament than the night before. Sofie looked at Ernstine and rolled her eyes in disgust at her brother's behavior.

With breakfast finished, Victor rose to engage his day. "C'mon, boy," he said gruffly to Ernst. "Let's go get the horses." Then he laughed openly as Ernst clenched his arms around his mother's leg. He knew that the horses frightened Ernst.

"Victor!" Sofie rebuked. The man laughed all the harder. Knowing he had succeeded in scaring his boy and angering his sister, he bellowed louder and louder as though gaining a victory for manliness. He looked enormous to Ernst as his body plugged the doorway then disappeared down the steps to the lower level. The atmosphere in the kitchen lightened as everyone sighed in relief.

It wasn't long before Sofie returned to lamenting being childless.

When his aunt left, Ernst watched as she walked several blocks down the dirt road to her home. Then he took surprising and sudden action—unimaginable for such a young boy. He went to his third floor bedroom, grabbed his pillow and went downstairs. His mother, who was gathering dirty laundry, took no notice as he headed through the outside door.

Clutching his pillow as though cuddling a friend, he leaped from foot to foot, imagining himself landing in his aunt's footsteps. Within five minutes he was knocking on her door.

"Ernst!" Sofie exclaimed as she looked down upon the tiny vagrant.

"I come live with you," he said in an eggshell-thin voice that flowed like soothing oil over her heart.

"Oh, Ernst, what are you saying, dear? Does your mother know you are here?"

She put her hand over her mouth as he shook his head no. *What will Ernstine think?* she wondered. *Surely she will not permit this.* Ernst's fragile voice had stirred maternal passion within her. It was frightening to be so close to mothering the lad only to think of him being torn away from her.

"First, let me get you a glass of milk, then we will go and talk with your mother." Ernst was too innocent and naive to perceive Sofie's fears. A desperate hope prompted her to leave his pillow at her home, then they ascended the grade to see Ernstine.

They entered the street level door and went up the stairs into the large kitchen. Along the inner wall were the cooking area, cabinets and a long settee where Ernstine often sat with her children laughing and singing. Against the back wall, before a wide window, was a thick-legged table surrounded by benches and chairs. The three sat at the table.

Sofie glanced at the red tulips outside the window, cleared her throat, scratched a phantom itch on her neck and began. "Ernstine, little Ernst came to my door and said that he would like to come live with me." She grinned and added, "He even brought his pillow."

A long silence followed. Sofie felt her heart pounding. She was certain the silence was her sister-in-law's way of preparing to tell her that this could not happen, that her boy belonged in his own home.

But, in fact, Ernstine was reflecting upon the emotional brutality of the previous night, and of the many nights before that as well. She trembled to think of the effect of that brutality on her young son.

"It would not be as though he were leaving me," she said wistfully. Sofie felt blood rushing to her head. "After all, you live just around the corner, and this village is like one big family anyway. Further, you did nothing to influence him toward this decision. I know this will be an important point, should Victor agree. Are you sure you want to do this?"

Swallowing a burst of excitement, Sofie composed herself and said, "Ernstine, you know that I love Ernst and will give him a good home."

"Yes, yes, I know that." Ernstine rubbed her hand over her tired brow. "You must be forewarned, however, that even at this young age Ernst has a mind of his own. You can see that in his decision to show up on your doorstep with his pillow. He won't be an easy child to raise, though I have very high hopes for him."

"I promise to do my best to see him become the man you want him to be."

Ernstine sighed deeply, stared out the window for a long while, then said, "All right, you take my Ernst with you."

The two women sealed the agreement with an embrace. Both wept, each feeling pain but from a different source. Ernst couldn't understand this profound emotion. He just slipped his hand into his aunt's and walked with her back to her home—back to his pillow.

CHAPTER TWO

The Boy and His Dog

Reaching over Ernst, Sofie opened the door for him to enter his new home. Suddenly, his face was slapped by a large, wet tongue that obliterated all light. It was Rico, the Saint Bernard that would become his best friend.

Ernst squealed with ear-splitting delight and immediately climbed onto Rico's back for a ride. Sofie held Ernst's arm, and Rico began his new role as a pony for the little boy. They frolicked through the house and were returning to the living room when they came to an abrupt halt. There stood his uncle—a tall man, quiet and firm—the final test of whether or not this would be Ernst's new home.

"Ernst has come to live with us," Sofie announced and then held her breath, hoping for a positive response. But there was only silence. The room froze.

Then Uncle Ernst, who was not given to open emotion, smiled, patted the boy's head and said, "I'm glad." A celebration erupted.

Ernst soon found that the spirit in this home was lighter than in his parents' home. His uncle, who rarely used alcohol, had a consistent disposition: silent, strong, reliable, kind. Also, Ernst was the only child in the household, so he was soon spoiled. He didn't have to share anything with his brothers or sister. And now he had more than his pillow—he had his friend Rico. While he missed the brightness of his mother's spirit, on most days he would run up the street to beg a cookie from her and always one for Rico too.

Each noon Uncle Ernst would come home from his work at the post office, eat lunch and then sleep for half an hour in the living room. Rico was not permitted on the sofa but was given a pillow to use as he flopped down on the floor to join the siesta. After a few big sighs, both were deeply asleep. As they rested, Sofie washed the dishes, then returned to her in-home work as a seamstress. Ernst felt secure.

Often Ernst would sit in the backyard and run his fingers through Rico's soft red and white hair, confiding in the wisdom of the dog's deep silence. "Rico, I love you. I will never ever leave you. I'll take you with me wherever I go. I promise to take care of you." His conversation meandered like a lazy stream, and Rico looked at him as though he understood.

Days passed, then years—five to be exact. Ernst was seven. He barely noticed that Rico was walking slower, nor did he realize that his dog breathed more heavily when he climbed the stairs. So he found it confusing the day he discovered Rico laying flat, not lifting his head. Ernst got on his knees beside his friend and coaxed, "C'mon, Rico, get up . . . get up. Let's play." But Rico only whimpered.

Aunt Sofie and Uncle Ernst were gripped by pain as they watched their little boy with his dog. Aunt Sofie cleared the lump in her throat, then said softly, "Rico doesn't feel well, son."

"But I want him to get up. What's wrong?" Ernst lamented.

"Rico is old," said Uncle Ernst. "He may not be with us too much longer."

"No, no. Get up, Rico," Ernst pled. "You'll be OK. I'll be with you." Ernst pulled Rico's head onto his lap and rocked on his knees. The dog shook as his shoulders rose and fell with each labored breath. Ernst tried to be brave, but then came the liquid rush of a breaking heart. Not wanting his nephew to see Rico's final breaths, Uncle Ernst carefully lifted the limp animal and carried him out of the house. Aunt Sofie placed her hands on the boy's trembling shoulders, knowing deep inside that his perfect world of bliss was abruptly ending.

That night, Ernst found comfort by laying his head on his old pillow. But it couldn't breathe or listen or run or care like Rico. He stared at the moon shining through his window. He still had his aunt and uncle, mother and father, brothers and sister. But there was a terrible sense of aloneness—something he hadn't known before. He was sure he could never love anyone as he loved Rico, nor would anyone else understand him so well.

Ernst was too young to know that the outside world was unraveling around him. Though there was a remnant of faithful pastors preaching biblical truth, many German theologians were turning from faith to rationalism—the belief that all truth is in man who, in turn, can control all things by sheer reason. Faith was belittled as a crutch for the feeble-minded. Anyone too vibrant in faith was considered fanatical.

In Berlin forty-seven-year-old Adolf Hitler, now in his third year of chancellorship, was forcefully speaking hope into the vacuum of despair the Germans had felt ever since losing World War I. The economy was bad, unemployment high and subjugation oppressive. The tinder was dry, ready for a lightning bolt of either good or evil to strike and set the nation ablaze. No one could detect that behind Hitler's promise to restore Germany's honor lay one of the worst evils ever to be unleashed across Europe.

But Ernst was oblivious to all of this. He was consumed by one thing alone—the collapse of his universe. Vast questions crowded into his little head, questions that no child's mind can resolve. How could God allow his best friend to die? Would life ever be happy again? His pillow absorbed his tears as his voice quivered, "I love you, Rico. I'll never forget you. I promise . . ." Then, nursing a deep ache in his chest, he fell asleep.

Adjustment came slowly. Loyalty caused Ernst to cling tenaciously to his memories of Rico, but time rudely shoved him into the future. The lesson was unmistakable: Life can be heartless toward childhood innocence. In time his laughter returned, but a wariness was born. A subconscious wall of self-protection, designed to keep out future pain, rose higher around his heart. The wall had been built much earlier while coping with the trauma of an alcoholic father, but now, Rico's death made the wall thicker and higher. Ernst's congenial disposition could swing suddenly to dark moods, making him as unpredictable as his future.

CHAPTER THREE

Ripe for the Reich

Although Ernst was too young to understand, apocalyptic days had come for Germany. The fiery-tongued Hitler was stirring the nation's Teutonic pride and national ambition to be strong and victorious once again.

Foreign intrusions from without and democratic deadlock from within angered the nation and left people without jobs. The time was ripe for an unwaveringly strong voice to say, "Enough!" That voice found a response in millions of languishing hearts ready to do anything to regain the rights to their homeland.

On September 1, 1939, Germany invaded Poland and war was declared. News of the war's outbreak splashed across the headlines, while the hope of victory flooded the German soul.

"Blood and Honor" became the slogan that inflamed the young. "Meine Jugend [my youth]" Hitler compelled with parental-sounding passion to the thousands of youth who packed stadiums, rigidly stretching their right arms forth in loyalty. Strength coursed through the nation's veins as Germany united before a common enemy.

The fresh wind of national pride swept all the way to the small village of Goenningen, causing a tornadic swirl of excitement behind the walled heart of ten-year-old Ernst. While he didn't understand his country's past, his youthful idealism awaited a call to purpose. God was not yet real to his heart. He sought identity. It came. Its name? The Third Reich. Its voice? Adolf Hitler. Ernst's heart blazed in response to the purpose represented by Hitler and his call for national unity.

For the next four years cities, towns and villages were slowly drained of young men who were needed on the front lines of war. All of the parents were consumed with concern for their sons' safety but proud that they were serving their Fatherland. Constant reports of victories bolstered their spirits.

During early March 1943, on the eve of his fourteenth birthday, Ernst was called to his parents' home. A teacher was visiting to confront them with a decision about Ernst's future. Sitting with Victor and Ernstine in the rarely used living room, the teacher began, "I think your son has the ability to be a teacher. I would like to see him go to the Napola."

"What will I gain from that?" Ernst boldly asked.

The teacher answered, "Keep in mind that this school is owned by the National Socialist German Workers' Party [NSDAP]. You will gain a complete education at no expense to you. You will be treated well . . . considered among the finest. Above all, you will serve the Reich." That was the final clarion call.

"I'll go," said Ernst. Ernstine and Victor agreed, knowing they could never afford to provide such an education for Ernst otherwise.

The school was in Esslingen, a town near Stuttgart. There Ernst would be enrolled in a six-year plan. The first years would complete his high school education, followed by a college curriculum. He would then graduate with an honorable position in the Third Reich.

Returning to his aunt and uncle's home, Ernst could barely contain his excitement. Within weeks he was stuffing clothes into a cloth sack to depart for Esslingen. Aunt Sofie offered her help while trying to conceal the ache in her heart.

Once packed, Ernst ran up to his parents' home. "Mom! . . ." he yelled as he entered the street-level door, then leaped two steps at a time to the second floor. His mother was sitting at the kitchen table, staring forlornly out of the window.

"Do you want something to eat?" Ernstine asked, attempting a smile. She was heartsick to think of his leaving, and frightened by the rapacious appetite of the German war machine. Would she ever see her son again?

"No, Mom, I just came to say good-bye." His voice sounded strong, like a conquering knight about to put the world aright.

Knowing better, his mother said only a soft, "Please, take care, my son . . . please take care of yourself." Her voice trailed off.

Then as suddenly as he came, he was gone. Ernstine bit her lip to stop the quivering. Watching her son disappear around the corner, she pressed her face into her hands and sobbed.

Late that morning Ernst boarded the bus at the village square. He looked back to watch the place of his youth diminishing behind him. His eyes gazed at the past, but his heart was set on the future—a future with an endless horizon of opportunity and importance.

The bus went north and stopped in Reutlingen, where he transferred to a train. The world was getting bigger. Each clickety-clack of the steel wheels thrust him further north to Esslingen, into his future of promise. Though not traveling even 100 miles from home, he felt as though he was being thrust into eternity.

Before he knew it, he stood before a five-story structure, its walls made of stone plastered with cement and punctuated by large windows with shutters. Soon he was in the registrar's office, filling out papers and receiving instructions. "You will be awakened at 6 a.m. to go to the flagpole in the courtyard for exercises, after which you will prepare for breakfast, then class."

And that's exactly what happened every day. The wake-up bell rang precisely at 6 o'clock, sending a herd of feet thundering down the hallway to the courtyard. Ernst found his place in the group, faced the flag and snapped to attention. A commander from the NSDAP stood erect and spoke with unflinching force.

"Your parents have suffered poverty and oppression. We have been downtrodden long enough. Germany is now rising up to command its rightful glory. We are at war. We *will* win! You are the young men who will guide the future. It is for your families, as well as this nation, that you must prepare to direct the generations to come. Hitler is counting on you, his youth."

When he finished, several hundred arms stiffly stretched toward the commander as a thunderous "Heil Hitler!" echoed off the walls. Ernst's body shivered with excitement. Surely he was part of the most powerful and important time of all history. Dreams of changing the world suffused his being. He exercised with abandon, then practiced the stiff-legged marching step in the privacy of his room. When he was sure no one was around, he would look into a full-length mirror, stare into his own eyes, click his heels, extend his right arm and say, "Heil Hitler!" After all, someday he might actually be in the Fuehrer's presence, so he must be prepared.

The teachers of the school were not all members of the NSDAP. While they were excellent teachers, they were bound by the NSDAP to protect the young men from any influence that would detract from their reverential loyalty to Adolf Hitler. This was evidenced by the disdain shown toward the church located beside the school. The students were told never to attend it, so none did. The spirit of the Reich was in conflict with the Spirit of God, and Christianity was berated as useless. *Who needs God anyway?* questioned Ernst. Unwittingly, he was adding pride to the hurt and pain that formed the mortar in the ever-growing wall surrounding his heart. Then, one day, he added addiction.

"Hey, ya' wanna try a cigarette?" asked an upperclassman.

Ernst's big moment had come, like a rite of passage. He took the cigarette, hoping his fingers wouldn't shake. He then put it between his lips, raised his chin and squinted the way he saw others do. Watching the lit match come toward the cigarette brought a mysterious thrill. The end glowed brightly, then dimmed as Ernst inhaled. Whack! It felt like a two-by-four smacked him right across the chest. He coughed and gagged, took another drag, then coughed some more. And so it was that Ernst coughed and gagged his way into manhood.

It wasn't long before Ernst could lean against a wall, prop one foot behind him, drag deeply and exhale a stream of smoke into the air. Day after day, he leaned on his new crutch of identity. The lad from Goenningen felt like a man shaping a new future for Germany, Europe and, perhaps, the world. Certainly, Hitler could rely on him to do anything. Ernst was ripe for the Reich.

Only a few short months after Ernst arrived at Esslingen, however, a mysterious darkness settled across the land.

CHAPTER FOUR

Ruin of the Reich

"**A**ir raid!" someone yelled as a siren pierced the calm air. The students poured down the stairwell to an underground shelter. Germany's newfound hope was crumbling. Hitler had driven his war machine too far. He miscalculated in two areas: First, his troops were hopelessly thinned across the vastness of Russia. Second, and far worse for Hitler, the United States—in addition to England and France—had officially entered the war. His euphoric belief that he could conquer the world soon evaporated. Hitler was overextended, overpowered and virtually alone.

All this, however, was shielded from Hitler's Youth. They were not frightened at first by the roar of bombers going overhead, sure that the German anti-aircraft would shoot down the allied troops. But nerves wore thin as the air raids occurred with increased frequency.

Then, one morning the sky was blackened by hundreds of bomber planes. Soon the deep drone of engines gave way to the percussive explosion of bombs dropping on nearby Stuttgart. Within the hour, brakes screeched as a large canvas-covered truck squealed to a stop before the school.

"Get in the truck!" barked an NSDAP commander urgently. The students scrambled onto the truck, which lurched forward and rushed to Stuttgart. Upon arrival, the truck stopped near a crater amid the buildings. Ernst choked on the acrid smoke rising from the grim holes where buildings had once stood. Some people roamed the streets in a daze; others scurried about, panic-stricken as they searched for lost loved ones.

"Get out of the truck!" came the next order. "These people need help. Dig through the rubble to find anyone who is wounded or dead. Cover the dead ones with a blanket, then pile the debris in that vacant lot over there. Move out! Now!"

A sick feeling gripped Ernst as he lifted boards, cement slabs and beams. Would he reach under something and feel a hand? Despairing groans and cries came from beneath the rubble. The students worked hard to reach people before it was too late. This became the grizzly routine for weeks, then months, even into the deep cold of winter.

"Ernst, why do you keep coughing?" asked one of his classmates following one such trip to Stuttgart, where biting winds swirled about their heads, ripped into their uniforms and chilled them to the bone.

"I don't know," Ernst replied between gasps. "But I can't stop. My chest hurts every time I cough."

"You better tell the school nurse."

"Yeah, I think I will. This isn't going away."

Following a medical examination, Ernst was called into the nurse's office for the report.

"I do not have good news for you, Ernst. I wish I could say you had bronchitis or pneumonia, but I'm afraid you have tuberculosis."

"TB?" Fear flashed through Ernst's heart. "What do I do about it?"

"Stay in bed. Keep as warm as you can. We'll give you a little extra bread and butter. That's all we can do. We'll wait and see if it improves."

Benumbed, Ernst went to his room, where he crawled into bed, wrapped the blankets tightly around his head and wept. Completely alone in his trouble, he lay there for days. Eventually, he continued his schooling while hacking, spitting blood and wondering if he'd ever see his family and friends again. Slowly he recovered, but the disease left a hole in one of his lungs.

Throughout 1944 insecurity spread across the land. Enemy bombers regularly dropped payloads on the Fatherland. The many trips to the air-raid shelter, followed by rummaging through the ruins of Stuttgart, eroded morale. Paranoia wrapped its fingers around the national psyche, though none dared voice their thoughts openly. The assuring rhetoric of Hitler was being drowned by the flood of death. Not only were Jews disappearing without explanation, but other mysterious disappearances occurred as well: Christian ministers, young people with physical problems, old and impaired people—all Germans, all vanishing. Villagers were simply told that they had passed away, but they were never told how.

All this caused Ernst, now fifteen years old, to think more deeply. Indeed, his shiny government shoes, crisp brown uniform and red Hitler Youth armband boasted of promise, but too often the blood he had to wash from it was German, not enemy. They ate well, but meat was becoming scarce. The pride Hitler instilled with his powerful speeches was sagging under the weight of reality.

One day, early in 1945, Ernst sat at his desk staring out the window. Snow fell quietly from the gray sky. The swirling, dancing flakes made Ernst sleepy. Then, suddenly, the class was snapped to attention as an NSDAP commander entered the room and sternly said, "You are all now sixteen. It's time to sign up for the military."

Ernst did not have to be asked twice. If ever the Reich had a devoted heart, it was Ernst's. He readily signed for a special unit, the paratroopers, and could hardly wait to be part of the blitz that would give Germany her final victory.

But it was a short-lived dream. "Sorry, son, you have been rejected from military involvement," said a commander.

Ernst was devastated. "What's wrong?" His voice was fragile, and he was on the verge of tears.

"Tuberculosis. You can't serve with that hole in your lung."

Thus Ernst was released from military service.

Then came Germany's collapse. As Western Allied forces crossed the Rhine, the head of the school gathered the students together for a final announcement: Burn all clothing that would identify them with the Third Reich. Burn all documentation that could associate them with the school. Go home. It was all over; Germany had lost the war.

Too numb to speak, Ernst stared, choked with disbelief. Hitler had infused youthful idealism with confidence. "No more oppression!" they had heard him promise. Hitler's dream had become a national agenda. The Germans never intended to follow an evil man; they merely wanted a leader who would empower a broken people.

On April 22, 1945, shortly after Ernst's sixteenth birthday, he made the sixty-mile trip back to Goenningen. His dreams had been destroyed by the very man who had awakened them.

The wall surrounding Ernst's heart thickened again as the events of his life to this point took their toll. Alcoholism had barred him from a good father-son relationship. Rico, his boyhood friend, had been ripped from him by death. Now betrayal spoke through the voice that had called the nation to pride and then reduced it to humiliation.

And the worst still lay ahead.

CHAPTER FIVE

Mistaken Identity

Ernst got off the bus and walked to his aunt and uncle's home. He had been to Armageddon and back—and that without victory. Trust had been violated. Hopes dashed. Having seen squalor on the streets of Stuttgart as people scavenged for food, he realized that his countrymen had been led to the mountain of victory and then shoved over the cliff of defeat. All was surreal as poverty fed upon poverty. A changed Ernst had returned home.

"Ernst . . . come, let me make you something to eat," greeted his aunt. His uncle would soon be home from work. There was virtually no conversation. What was there to discuss? The whole nation was numb, silent and afraid. Ernst and Sofie just ate, thankful to be together.

After they finished, Ernst went to see his parents. He trudged up the steps past the barn and entered the kitchen. His throat felt tight; he didn't know what to say. His mother's fears had proven more valid than his confidence. The opportunity to win his father's attention by becoming someone important was gone. As he sat down, Ernst's mother ran her fingers through his hair. Victor joined the subdued wake. What do we do now? was the question hanging in the air. In time Ernst's sister and brothers gathered in the kitchen, all saying nothing. The silence was a statement of despair.

Life had never offered Ernst a sense of security, and now the bottom had fallen out. Berlin was a snarl of crushed walls and twisted metal. Bomb craters pocked the streets. Hitler's body lay in front of his bunker, charred beyond recognition. One fatal, self-inflicted bullet had silenced the brain that had masterminded hell on earth. Now, a powerless nation was forced to bow before an unmerciful world. Germany was racing toward full surrender. Bare-bones survival was on everyone's mind.

One morning Ernst joined his father and uncle in the village pub, where many gathered to discuss the doom that had befallen their nation. "I just returned from Berlin last night and saw the destruction," stated one of the men. "It's beyond belief."

"So, what's going to happen now?" asked another.

The town's mayor responded, "There are four powers who will control the country: Russia, Great Britain, France and the United States. The Americans and English will be civil. The French will be ruthless and the Russians far worse. Unfortunately, our sector is under French control. You must hide everything, especially your wives and daughters. It's going to be bad."

His words were prophetic. The French soldiers had just been given two days to round up German soldiers who were hiding in their homes and, in the process, do anything else they wanted. A frenzy of rape, murder and plunder spewed forth like liquid fire from a dragon's mouth.

Someone in the pub yelled, "I hear them shooting! The French troops are close." The mayor's words were still gripping Ernst's mind. *My clothes and credentials*, he thought.

They must not discover that I was at a Hitler school. Who knows what they will do? He ran from the pub to his aunt and uncle's home. Palms sweating, he gathered his school uniform, armband and credentials, then ran down to the backyard where he built a fire that quickly destroyed all association with the Third Reich. Watching his promised future turn to ashes, he sensed an inaudible voice speaking from behind the wall in his heart, "Betrayed again. Abandoned. Violated. Alone. Life did it again. And where is God?" He scattered the ashes, then turned and went into the house for lunch.

Uncertainty sat at the table with them. Ernst was about to take a bite of his sandwich when there came an angry pounding at the door. Uncle Ernst got up and opened the door. There stood two black French soldiers from the French-governed region of Senegal in Africa. They entered the home and walked past Uncle Ernst as though he were merely a statue.

"You!" one said pointing at Ernst. "You German soldier? You hiding in civilian clothes?" He barely spoke German, making communication difficult.

Drained of strength, Ernst replied, "No. I am just a civilian, a student. I'm only sixteen."

"Liar!" the soldier thundered. Ernst had no idea if the soldier was as fierce as he sounded. For all Ernst knew, he would be shot. His uncle and aunt tried to intervene for Ernst, assuring the soldier that their nephew was telling the truth.

"Shut up!" the soldier ordered. "He's lying. Look, that's him in picture. Stop lying. You are a soldier." Ernst turned to see a picture of his older brother Horst in his soldier's uniform hanging directly behind him on the wall. Horst was missing in Russia, but Ernst realized that in the picture Horst looked just like him.

Feeling weaker, Ernst tried to explain. "No, no. That's not me. That's my older brother. He has been missing ever since he entered Russia with the German army."

"It's true," assured Uncle Ernst and Aunt Sofie.

"Enough lies! That's you!" barked the soldier. He went to the other soldier and spoke in French to him. The second soldier left. Then the spokesman stood by the front door, not letting the three leave his sight. It felt like they were on death row. No words were exchanged. No assurance offered. That small soldier was suddenly in powerful command and was treating the situation as though he were a little god.

"What's happening?" Sofie gently asked. Her question fell into silence. The soldier continued watching them, glancing occasionally at the street outside until the other soldier returned an hour later.

"You!" the commanding one said pointing at Ernst. "Outside!" The hair on Ernst's neck bristled from fear as he walked past the soldier. Was this his execution? Outside he saw a large truck filled with German soldiers standing shoulder to shoulder. Some of the prisoners were from his village. There were eighty in all. "Get on!" demanded the Senegalese soldier. One prisoner leaned down and extended his arm. Ernst grabbed his hand and felt himself being lifted onto the truck. The weathered soldier looked at Ernst, then, turning to another soldier, he grunted and said, "Just a boy. Who will they take next?"

The truck remained parked as the French soldiers searched Ernst's aunt and uncle's home, hoping to pillage valuables. Ernst swallowed deeply, hoping they would not find his passport and government shoes hidden in the ceiling. He noticed some soldiers sporting stolen watches from their wrists to their shoulders. Anything that glittered was looted.

Finally, the uncivil victors felt sure they had everything and jumped onto the truck. A black cloud of smoke swirled from the exhaust as the truck jolted forward. By that time, Ernst's parents had heard of the events and arrived at the scene. Ernst lifted his hand to wave good-bye to his relatives, who were helpless to save him. His only comfort was in thinking that his mother and aunt were too old for the soldiers to want to rape, but he was worried for his sister's safety. He had heard of young women sleeping in the forest so as not to be attacked by the Frenchmen. Uncle Ernst, having faced his own horrors as a prisoner of war (POW) during World War I, was choked by emotion as he watched Ernst disappear.

The lad who had watched the village diminish from a bus that took him into a boundless future now watched it diminish from the back of a truck taking him to prison. Because of mistaken identity, Ernst Vatter had become a prisoner of a war he had not asked for, but one that was about to show him the worst degradation of the human heart.

CHAPTER SIX

Life in the Evil Abyss

Ernst recognized some villagers among the prisoners but gained no comfort from their presence. There was no camaraderie; he was younger than the rest and had not been in the military. While he had seen the aftermath of the bombings, he had never stared down the barrel of an enemy gun. These prisoners bore a hardness that came from the trenches of combat.

"Look, kid," one said, "don't be scared. We'll make it." Ernst nodded, then looked back to the valley that cradled his home.

The truck bounced and rumbled northward for an hour until it stopped in Tuebingen where it was met by soldiers with guns raised. "Get down! Get down!" came the order. Ernst jumped off the truck and saw a massive building surrounded by a steel fence to his right. It was a German barracks. "March into that building!" was the next command. The very building that had been home to some of Hitler's troops was now their prison, at least for that first night.

The motley group was herded into the barracks, filling the many rooms and hallways already clogged with prisoners. The evening wore long and lonely with no meal and little talk. All felt insecure and defenseless, surrounded by Senegalese with guns. Ernst noticed one younger man singled out and taken away, then another. In time they returned.

The first one sat beside Ernst, trembling, but said nothing. He started to whimper. Ernst looked away to give the man privacy. Finally the man spoke in a shaky whisper to Ernst. "Do you know what that one over there did to me? He used me."

"He what? What do you mean?"

The man cursed, then added, "He raped me, that filthy. . . ." He fell silent, dripping with shame. Suddenly the quietness was shattered by a man's scream . . . then another long scream from the same man, then another. A door opened and a German soldier stumbled into the room holding his hand over his mouth. His eyes stared a thousand yards into nothing. He sat down to avoid fainting and, removing his hand from his mouth, he spit a pool of fresh blood onto the floor.

"What happened? What did they do to you?" asked a prisoner who knew him.

"They ripped two teeth out of my mouth. . . ." He replied, swearing freely.

"What are you saying? Why?"

"The gold. They wanted the gold in my teeth."

He rolled up his shirt and clamped his jaws tight on it to stop the bleeding. The other men sat paralyzed as another was led out at gunpoint. A loud terrifying scream followed. He was returned as another was escorted out. This went on for some time.

Ernst tried to get comfortable on the floor. A large Senegalese guard lay down beside him and soon fell asleep, but Ernst stayed awake the entire night, traumatized by the lurking evil.

The next morning 300 hungry prisoners were marched thirty-five miles west to Nagold. Ernst's last meal had been the sandwich that had nearly stuck in his throat when the soldiers pounded on the door of his home the day before. His stomach made a growling demand as they passed a bakery, but the freedom to eat was gone.

The prisoners were put into a quarry and kept under the open sky for two days and nights. The gruff roar of diesel engines was heard the third day as trucks backed up to the quarry.

"Get on!" came the sharp command, and the men climbed onto the trucks. Destination? Knielingen, a town on the edge of Karlsruhe. The spring wind whipping through Ernst's hair felt free, but it was powerless to save him from sinking ever more deeply into hopelessness. He found himself envying the freedom of the cattle they passed in the fields.

"Get off!" came the next command when they arrived at Knielingen. As Ernst jumped down from the truck, he saw a huge door open wide, waiting to swallow them all. It was an unheated cement tank garage surrounded by a high fence laced with barbed wire. A loosely coiled strand of razor wire hung atop the fence. In front of the building was a fenced courtyard. Towers surrounded the compound, making escape impossible.

"Hey," barked a soldier looking directly into Ernst's eyes. "Take off those shoes!"

Ernst was glad that his good government-issued shoes were hidden as he unlaced his worn shoes and drew his feet out. He watched as the soldier tied the laces together and flung them over his shoulder. They were now his.

"Enter!" shouted a soldier. The cold cement floor was covered with straw. The grim walls were barely lit by five lightbulbs dangling from the ceiling. It was time for instructions.

"Take care of the straw because that's all you're going to get for a long time. There will be one meal a day—one piece of bread and some corn. That oil barrel in the middle of the floor is your toilet. Each morning two of you will empty it, so plan to take turns. You'll be fed tomorrow." Then the doors were slammed shut.

Disoriented, the men began talking quietly to one another. Nerves unraveled. "Get out of here or I'll kill you!" yelled one man as he fought with another over some straw. Ernst slumped to the floor in disbelief. Fresh air and freedom were gone, and now he was trapped in a building with men on the outer edge of sanity.

Hungry, depressed and confused, he curled up in some straw and fell asleep. He awoke hours later. The deep blackness was softened only by one dim light hanging in the center of the room. Ernst assumed it was the middle of the night. The stench of excrement filled his throat, and he felt the urge to wretch. He swallowed, but the pungent foulness remained. He opened his eyes to see a man sitting on the oil barrel relieving himself.

Many men had been to the barrel over the previous hours. The putrid air was mingled with cursing as the contents of the barrel spilled over, running under the straw of prisoners lying nearby. Pushing back, these men, in turn, crowded others. Threats were made.

Ernst locked his fingers behind his head and stared up into nothingness. Nostalgia took him by the arm and walked him deep into his past. Soon he was transported in sweet thought, forgetting for the moment the strangling odor of the building. He envisioned his mother laughing and singing. He smelled muffins baking over the fire. Then his thoughts shifted to his aunt and uncle's home: the love, the safety, the respect. He thought of lying in his bed with his pillow.

The scene changed. He was a little boy again. He felt the warm sun and cool breeze as he ran with Rico high up on the mountain behind his home. He could see forever from that mountain. Frolicking and running, he laughed. "Rico, come boy! C'mon, Rico, let's run some more," he called out in his hallucination.

Suddenly, there came a gruff, "Shut up, kid." Ernst was abruptly returned to reality. Hot tears ran down his cheeks. He bit his lip, trying to quiet the desperate longing of his soul.

Early the next morning the large doors were opened. Ernst could almost see the fresh air replace the stench. Two men carried the overflowing barrel to a dump. "Everybody outside," came the order. Three hundred men poured into the fenced courtyard where they received their meal: one piece of bread and one ear of field corn each. Not sweet corn, just hard field corn—the kind fed only to animals.

"Try to eat slowly, kid," said one prisoner to Ernst. "You'll feel like you're eating more that way. Snap the kernels off and chew them slowly. That way you'll shorten the gap between meals and your stomach won't ache as much later."

After they received a drink of water, the day slogged down into lying around and talking about nothing. Periodically the thought of the doors being shut again, enclosing the men around the barrel in the middle of the floor, caused Ernst to nearly vomit. But that would be his future, day after day, night after night.

Within a week, hunger felt like an animal trying to gnaw its way out of his body. The men's faces became gaunt. Some stepped beyond sanity and started babbling nonsense. Violent fights broke out over a scrap of food or a fistful of straw. Ernst watched men who were doctors, lawyers and business owners, all acting equally crazed. His admiration for position and titles died.

Then one day the most unexpected thing happened, revealing a different side of humanity seen in only a few.

"My name is Robert Vatter," said a middle-aged prisoner, extending a hand of friendship.

"Is that so?" Ernst curtly replied. "Vatter is my name, too, though surely we're not related."

"No, probably not. I just want to ask you a question: Are you hungry?"

Ernst swore. "What kind of a question is that? We're only getting one piece of bread and one ear of that lousy corn each day, and you ask if I'm hungry. Of course. I'm starving."

"Well, starting tomorrow I will give you one-half of my piece of bread. You are young and need it more than I do."

"How can you do that? Are you able to steal some?"

Robert pulled a thin Bible out of a pocket in his torn coat and said, "No, I will steal nothing. The Lord Jesus Christ will help me do it."

From the next day forward Ernst ate one and a half pieces of bread, plus an ear of corn. The impact of this unconditional, selfless love rammed against the wall surrounding his heart. But by that time the young man was so confused and embittered that the wall barely budged. As days passed and Robert stayed true to his word, Ernst thought, *If that's what a true Christian is, I wish I could be like that man.*

One day, while in the courtyard, a prisoner asked, "Ernst, do you know who occupies those tall buildings over there, the ones where the windows are barred?"

"No."

"Some of the Nazi leaders who were in charge of villages and towns. They'll probably face execution," he said in a tone of cold reality that held no trace of regret.

Ernst looked at the windows and thought, *Just over there are the men who caused me to be here. They tried to conquer the world with might and lost. Their strength cannot compare to Robert's: strength rooted in a Power within that makes him completely different.*

Several days later, there was a loud scuffle in the courtyard as soldiers wrestled a prisoner to the ground. An older man, whom Ernst recognized as being from his village, had walked too close to the fence, gesturing as though to climb over it. He may have been hallucinating, since he was too weak to escape anyway. Still, the soldiers took this opportunity to make a grand display of power. A decision was made to execute the man at 10 o'clock the next morning. The stench-filled garage was exceedingly quiet throughout the night.

At 10 o'clock sharp the prisoners were lined up and stripped to the waist to watch the slaying. Then the leader shouted at the blindfolded man to face the wall.

"Ready!" Six soldiers raised their rifles to their shoulders.

"Aim!" The six pressed their cheeks against their rifle stocks. Closing one eye, they squinted with the other, sighting the prisoner's heart in the cross hairs. The pause seemed eternal.

"Fire!" The prisoner dropped to the ground and lay motionless, though he was still breathing. No shots were heard. Only six clicks. The guns weren't loaded. The commander then turned to the prisoners and warned sternly: "Let this be a lesson to all of you. This time I am showing mercy, but if any one of you tries to escape again, the guns *will* be loaded. You *will* be shot! Dismissed."

Ernst looked at the man lying on the ground, thinking that he had surely had a heart attack. To everyone's surprise, however, he had not—he had simply dropped from extreme fright.

Later, Ernst mustered the nerve to ask him, "Do you mind telling me what you thought about as you stood expecting to die?"

"My wife and children," replied the man. Then, following a long pause, he added, "Life, I thought about life."

There was no more commentary. Ernst didn't feel free to pursue the matter any further. But he realized that he, too, was beginning to think about that exact same thing—life. Arrested because of mistaken identity, he was in a place that stripped him of all self-respect and identity. He wondered who he was, what he was. His only touch with what it meant to be a human was Robert. He clung to that thread of hope.

Still, the pendulum of threat didn't stop swinging above his head.

CHAPTER SEVEN

Bridge to Nowhere

One morning, as usual, the large wooden doors opened to disgorge the foul odor, the excrement and the men. Ernst stood in the repugnant breeze thinking, *How is it possible that I still feel human in the middle of this? But I do. I feel human. I'm here, but this is not me. Hang on, Ernst. Survive. Stay alive.*

"Hey, Ernst," said a grubby man with a sagging belly. "Have you ever been with a woman? Let me tell you about this woman I was with in . . ."

"Shut up!" Ernst demanded with a curse. "This talk is as filthy as the stench from that barrel. I can't believe that my own countrymen are acting like this." Some men who overheard the exchange felt a pang of guilt. Ernst's reprimand reminding them of the moral moorings they had lost.

Sensuous talk certainly sounded intriguing and mysterious, but it was also frightening and disgusting. Ernst was a young man straight from a village of virtue dumped into a den of iniquity. Some had dragged immorality with them from large cities. Others had abandoned their moral training for the thrill of sexual conquest while invading other countries. This was true of all except Robert Vatter and a few others like him.

37

"Good morning, Ernst." It was Robert handing him this day's piece of bread.

"Thank you, Robert. Are you sure you can keep doing this?"

"I will continue until we are out of here. Don't worry, I'll be all right. The Lord will be faithful."

Ernst was fascinated by Robert. He preached with actions, not words. While Ernst didn't share Robert's personal faith, he admired the strength of it. Amid the dung pile of vile behavior, experiencing Robert's faith was like standing under a waterfall on a warm summer day. As they ate, Ernst found himself staring at Robert wondering, *What makes him this way?*

The day's routine of idle chatter in the courtyard was interrupted by a sharp command. "Take off your clothes!" barked a soldier. All stripped. Suddenly the prisoners felt their skin sting as large fire hoses were aimed at them. There was no soap, but at least there was water to wash some of the caked sweat from their bodies. They stood in the sun to dry.

"Get dressed," was the next order.

Ernst picked up his crusty clothes, thinking how soft they had been when he had put them on just three weeks earlier.

"Everyone, get on the trucks," came the third order. "You will be driven to Karlsruhe to clean up the streets." The thought of activity brought relief. Anything would be better than lying around for another day listening to wild war stories coupled with lurid details of escapades. And there were the fights. Nearly every day there was a fight resulting from hunger, boredom, frustration or fear. At least today there would be activity to sponge away the sense of despair.

"I'll need a pair of shoes," Ernst said to a soldier.

"Yeah, kid, you will." The soldier rounded up a Russian boot and a regular shoe. Two different shoes, two different sizes.

The gate was opened and the men, flanked by armed guards, boarded the trucks. Hearing the engines rev and smelling the diesel exhaust awakened hope of freedom. Simple freedom was all the heart cried for. *Oh,* thought Ernst, *if only I could brush my teeth again. And to sit and soak in a tub of hot water would feel so good. Ah, but at least we'll be doing something today, something besides stagnating in filth.*

Ernst faced the mild May wind as the trucks bolted northwest. He filled his lungs with deep gulps of air to capture the pure fragrance of the spring blossoms. He saw a stallion galloping across a meadow and thought, *How strange it is to be passing through such extraordinary freedom and yet be a prisoner.* The war could not enslave the world. Only humanity was enslaved.

He looked at the men on the truck, some with high education and many accomplishments. They proved to be as vulgar as the least educated, often wrangling over a bread crumb. The guards were certainly no better. Some had used prisoners to satisfy their own dark cravings. Ernst thought, *We're all prisoners. Something has us all bound. No one is different. One holds a gun, while the others cower, but all are the same. Some use big words and others don't, but in a crisis there is no difference. All except Robert. How does one become like Robert? It would really be something to be like him.*

An hour later the brakes screeched as the trucks stopped in Karlsruhe. "Everyone, get off! You will form teams of two. You will always be in sight of a guard. If anyone tries to escape, you will be shot dead without warning. You will put all the rubbish and debris in a pile at that intersection. A truck will come, and you will load it. At 6 o'clock you will be brought back here for our return."

So, fueled with one and a half pieces of bread and an ear of field corn, Ernst worked through the day with no future other than to lie down that night in his crusty clothes on dirty straw, trying to ignore the gagging odor and the painful sores on his feet from his mismatched shoes. Then he would listen; listen to men groaning, weeping and cursing. Laughter was rare and almost always suggestive.

Day after day, night after night, Ernst observed the two realities. He had a distaste for the one but admiration for the other. Suspended between the two he found himself most impressed by Robert.

Then one morning the doors creaked open like yawning craters, and the men emerged to a new experience. The trucks were being loaded for deportation. German prisoners were being taken from all over the country to Russia and France to be used in hard labor. They would become slaves. Fear gripped the men, realizing that some might never see their families again.

"Hello, Robert," Ernst said, as he pushed his way to the back of the truck to be with his friend.

"Good morning, lad."

"What's going to happen?"

"This is bad, but it should not affect you, Ernst. You are only sixteen. I know you told me that you are in here because of mistaken identity, but you are also here illegally. According to the Geneva Convention, no soldier under eighteen can be arrested."

"Really?"

"Yes, it's true."

"But these men are ignoring that. I'll probably be taken with all the rest."

"I pray not, lad . . . I pray not," he said with fatherly concern.

Ernst's stomach tightened as the trucks rumbled westward toward the Rhine, destined for France. Finally, just before crossing the emergency pontoon bridge to France, the trucks came to a halt. American soldiers surrounded them. A neatly clad commander in a well-pressed brown uniform saluted the French commander, then asked, "Who are these men?"

"German prisoners, sir."

"Where are you taking them?"

"To France, sir, by orders of the French command."

"Who up there is under eighteen years of age?" shouted the American to the prisoners.

"Here's one," Robert yelled pointing at Ernst. Several others were also identified. Ernst pushed to the edge of the truck to be sure his hand was seen.

"Get off the truck," commanded the American. "Empty one of these trucks to take these young men back to be released. It is forbidden to detain men of this age."

Ernst had never seen an American before. He studied everything about the commander: his eyes, jaw, voice and language. He looked at the others too. They seemed sane. Was Hitler's indoctrination about being superior to the world false? Were the degenerate men he was thrust among not the essence of humanity? Was there a bigger world than what he had known? These men seemed to be civil, without arrogance, even toward their enemies. The wall around his heart was once again being bombarded.

Ernst stared at the truck filled with German soldiers. Robert stood at the back, forcing a smile and waving to Ernst, who wondered, *Is this the last I'll ever see him? Why should such a good man be lost to slavery?* He waved back to the most impressive man he'd ever met. His last thought was, *How can I ever be like him?*

Soon Ernst was back at Knielingen, clad in his only possessions: the odd pair of shoes and the clothes that were now encrusted with three weeks of filth. But, at least he was free—released on a bridge to nowhere.

CHAPTER EIGHT

Bleeding Feet and Broken Dreams

Ernst jumped off the truck that returned them to the prison camp at Knielingen. Emerging from what seemed like a black hole of missing time, he asked an old man hobbling by, "What's today's date?"

"It's June 1." The man never looked at Ernst, just stated the date.

Ernst said, "Thank you," but the old man never acknowledged him. He simply shuffled on toward nothing, since his own little world of dreams had been gutted by the war too.

Ernst took a deep breath and smiled as he looked at the prison that was powerless to claim him this day. He felt like a knight placing his sword upon a slain dragon's heart. He was the victor!

The gloating was short-lived, however, when he realized the problems that lay before him. He was free from the prison, but a greater slavery engulfed him, one that ensnared the whole land. The entire nation had been taken hostage. French soldiers roamed about, ready to capture any former soldiers—even those who had been released by the American and British forces—to imprison them again and force them to labor in France. They even shot those who they felt were trying to escape. With a year of unharvested crops rotting in the fields and industry in shambles, poverty became the master of millions. Ernst realized that he had been released from one prison into another—a nightmare caused by the diabolic dreams of the very Fuehrer who had promised to lead Germany to freedom.

Terry Schultz and Helmut Heidelberg, two other teenagers from the village of Goenningen, had been released with Ernst. They all feared what they might find at home, but first they had to think of how to get there.

"We can't stay in the open or walk by day, or we'll be caught for sure," Ernst said to them. "We'll have to stay in the forest all the way home. Let's get up in that section of trees and hide until night, then we can start for home." The three trudged away from the prison to the nearby shelter of the Black Forest.

At last, atop a ridge, they stopped under a shield of trees to rest until nightfall. Ernst sat down, leaned against a stump and removed his shoes. There he was—just a teenager with bleeding feet and broken dreams.

Finally, it was 8 o'clock, dusky enough to safely continue their arduous trek. They had barely begun when Ernst sat down, holding his feet. "I don't know how I can make it. It feels as though I have broken glass in my shoes."

"C'mon, Ernst, get up. You have to. There's no other choice. If you're found, you might get shot. Who knows what they'll do to you," whispered Terry. Terry and Helmut lifted Ernst to his feet, and he tried to walk again. A root caught his right foot, pressing the shoe against an open sore. His eyes watered as he raised his chin and inhaled deeply. He dared not yell out. After a loud exhale he took another step, then another and another, hitching his shoulders with each step to absorb the pain. The three silhouettes moved slowly through the shadowy forest. Remaining on the ridge, they walked deep into the night but had no idea how many miles they traversed.

As they crested a hill, they saw the roof of a barn shining in the moonlight. "Let's try to get some sleep in that barn," said Helmut. "Hopefully, the farmer won't report us even if he finds us." So the trio stealthily walked down the hill to the barn, climbed into the hayloft and flopped backwards into the welcoming hay. Ernst gingerly removed his shoes, his feet throbbing with pain, but soon he was in a deep sleep.

They awakened to roosters crowing. The air in the loft was ghastly hot and humid, and their shirts were wet from perspiration. They heard no movement and could only hope they had not been discovered and reported.

"I'm hungry," said Terry.

"Me, too. I'm going to eat a whole cow when I get home," said Helmut. The other two grunted in agreement. When their stomachs began to growl, they decided to talk about other things.

Then . . . "Shhh!" warned Terry, pressing his finger across his lips. The three lay motionless in the loft as the barn door creaked open, and the farmer entered below. He spent what seemed like an eternity repairing a horse harness, and the boys felt their joints locking as they remained frozen. Finally, the farmer flung the harness over his shoulder and left.

Long morning shadows extended from the trees, inviting a quick return to the safety of the forest. "Let's go!" urged Helmut.

Ernst bit on a stick while pulling on his shoes. When he took his first step, he felt as though he had been shot in the foot. They climbed down the ladder, then slipped through the door and were swallowed in a flood of trees. Throughout the morning they slogged along, stopping often to wait for the pain in Ernst's feet to subside. When the sun was high and strong they rested and hid so they would not be spotted through a soldier's binoculars. The day proved to be as difficult as the previous one, except for the hope that each laborious step was one step closer to home.

Finally one evening, they sat down on the edge of the eastern slopes of the Black Forest, overlooking the village of Kuppingen. Spotting the steeple of a Lutheran church, Ernst said, "Let's go down to the pastor's home and stay there for the night. He's a Christian. He'll help us without turning us over to the French." All agreed. So, trying to hurry before being spotted by soldiers, they shuffled to the manse.

Ernst pounded on the door. No response. He pounded again, then again. Finally, a dim light appeared from a window near the door. The door swung open and the pastor, bewildered and frazzled, stood before them. He had been sleeping and wasn't pleased with the intrusion.

"Sir," said Ernst, "we were imprisoned by the French. They were deporting us when the Americans stopped the trucks at the pontoon bridge. When they were told we are under eighteen, they demanded our release. We were set free at the prison camp at Knielingen, and are trying to get to our home in Goenningen. We have been walking through the forest . . . up there," he said, pointing vaguely in the direction of the trees, " . . . along that ridge. We can't use the roadways or we could be shot."

"Yes, that's true," said the pastor. "Come in." By that time his wife was standing with her hand on his shoulder. She winced when she saw Ernst stumble.

"Oh, poor boy, what's wrong?" she questioned.

"My feet. They're covered with open sores from these shoes. They were given to me in prison so that I could work on the streets of Karlsruhe, but they don't fit. My feet have been rubbed raw ever since."

"Sit down here." She pointed to a chair in the kitchen. "First you boys must eat." Her voice was soft and kind like the cooing of a dove. She started a fire in the kitchen stove as the pastor—who had introduced himself as Erhard Eisenman—departed to collect some clean cloths and healing salve for Ernst's feet.

Ernst gingerly slid off his shoes. His feet throbbed, but he forgot the pain as his stomach responded to the alluring odor rising from the stove. The pastor's wife—"Call me Elizabeth," she had told them—was warming stew that the family had enjoyed earlier in the evening. His stomach yearned aloud. Soon, large bowls filled to the brim with piping hot chunks of beef, carrots, celery, potatoes and barley floating in thick brown gravy sat before them. The three scooped and gulped the food as the pastor and his wife looked on in amazement. Within minutes she refilled their bowls. Again they downed the contents, but in a slightly more polite fashion.

After they ate, Pastor Eisenman said, "I boiled some water for each of you to take a bath. You go first, Ernst, so that we can work on your feet." Ernst went into the bathroom and gently slipped into the tub of hot water. After scrubbing and drying, he hobbled to the kitchen and sat down.

Elizabeth studied his feet, then took a warm, damp cloth and dabbed the pus-filled sores. Ernst cringed, but resolved not to show weakness. She put a glob of salve on each sore and wrapped his feet in soft cloth. "There, I hope that will help you get home."

"Thank you," said Ernst. He went to bed without the disturbance of a gnawing stomach for the first time in weeks. His dreams were sweet, and he awakened before dawn with fresh hope. He shook Terry and Helmut.

"What's the matter with you, Ernst? Leave us alone," they complained.

"No, no, we must leave before it gets light. We cannot risk being seen in the streets." Jolted to their senses, they quickly dressed.

They heard Pastor and Mrs. Eisenman's footsteps in the hall. "We want to give you some breakfast before you go," said Elizabeth.

After each downed a large bowl of porridge, the boys headed toward the woods. Ernst wasn't limping as badly as before, since the salve and the soft cloth helped cushion his sores. Still, he walked carefully, knowing a long day lay before them. At day's end they found another barn in which to sleep.

Finally, they reached Goenningen. They fully expected to walk separately to their homes, but as soon as they were on the edge of the village, someone yelled, "Look! There's Helmut . . . and Ernst . . . and, and there's Terry!" Word spread like the scream of a siren. Villagers dropped their pitchforks and hoes and ran toward them.

Victor and Ernstine Vatter joined the flow of neighbors in the streets, Ernstine's dress billowing behind her as she ran. By then, Aunt Sofie and Uncle Ernst had also heard the news and emerged from their home as Ernstine and Victor ran by. Never before did the four look at each other with such delight.

The three lads stared at the tidal wave of humanity, puzzled to suddenly find themselves amid a sea of hugging arms. Pats fell on their backs from a hundred directions.

The villagers were transported into effusive expressions of joy to see the young men.

Ernstine pushed through the friendly mob, which parted for the mother to reach her son. She said nothing, just held him tightly. Soon Victor planted a gentle pat on his shoulder and said, "Glad you're home, son." Sofie placed her hand on his arm. Then came a great surprise. Uncle Ernst, that quiet man of deep self-control, was weeping. All the while Ernst was in prison, his uncle, who had known the horrid life of a POW, had brooded with concern. The sight of young Ernst safe at last broke his composure, and that without shame.

After the joyous homecoming, Ernst limped toward his aunt and uncle's home. He expected to enjoy a quiet dinner, but to his surprise, people kept coming to the house throughout the evening. He was humbled to see them bringing cakes and other delights they had prepared in his honor from their meager pantries. Voices were high-pitched from lighthearted excitement.

Ernst went to bed late that night. It felt good to be greeted by such affection, but a coldness lurked in his heart. Though hollow-eyed and haggard, Ernst looked the same. But he wasn't. The wall around his heart was higher and thicker than ever, and the drawbridge was tightly shut and locked. No one would be allowed in, and Ernst was not about to come out. This was not the Ernst that the village once knew. Nor did he feel that he knew himself anymore. He looked at his boyhood pillow that his aunt kept atop a dresser, but a hardness allowed no tender thought to return. Soft memories of Rico were reduced to cold fact. He lit a cigarette, took a deep drag and wondered if he had lost his soul.

Yet, while Ernst felt he had lost himself, he was not lost to God. Indeed, he was racing toward the most important encounter of his life.

CHAPTER NINE

The Long Night's War

The next morning, Ernst awakened to laughter rising from the kitchen. It was his mother and aunt giggling like two teenagers over having Ernst home. "We need to get some meat on his bones," he heard them saying to each other.

If they only knew what I've been eating, he thought. He looked into the mirror above his dresser. "Gaunt. You're a skinny wreck," he whispered to himself as he ran his fingers down his cheeks. "Why are they so happy? You were going to liberate Germany and return a hero. Now, Germany is in ruins and you come home a skeleton." His spirit darkened as he threw on some clothes and went downstairs, though his craving for a good breakfast overpowered his concerns.

"Good morning," his mother and aunt gushed.

"Good morning," he replied, his voice flat and sulky.

"What's wrong?" asked his mother.

He balked, then mumbled, "I guess I better get a job . . . but where . . . and how?"

"Oh, I'm afraid there are no jobs," sighed his aunt as she rubbed her neck.

"Everyone is struggling just to exist," confirmed his mother. "Just wait. Your time will come." Her smile exuded confidence.

With no destination in mind, Ernst ascended the mile-long climb to the top of Rossberg Mountain behind his home, where his father's horses were grazing. Sitting down to watch their manes blow freely in the breeze, Ernst wished he were as free, but his heart was imprisoned by his bitter response to the people and events that had plundered his life. He became increasingly morose.

He thought of the betrayal of the Third Reich and trembled. *How could they? How could they promise us so much, then destroy our dreams? What right do they have to play with lives in this way?* Faces of the French Senegal soldiers were riveted in his mind, setting his stomach aflame. He lit a cigarette and hoped the confusion and rage would rise with the smoke. They didn't. When the sun was a mere slit on the horizon, he descended the hill and went to bed.

* * *

The summer of 1945 blazed by slowly. No work. No way to dispel boredom. No cure for the sense of worthlessness that crept over him.

Weeks and months passed. One morning Ernst awakened to the odor of dry leaves burning in a neighbor's yard. His senses were struck by what his eyes failed to see. The colorful foliage was saluting the hot summer good-bye. The crisp air mantled his shoulders and ignited a special hunger.

"Ernst, are you ready for breakfast?" called Sofie.

"Am I ever! I'll be right down." He threw on his trousers and shirt and descended the steps like a leopard about to pounce upon its prey. His face disappeared as he bent over the bowl to devour the thick, hot porridge.

"Ernst?"

"Yeah," he managed to get out between gulps.

With great hesitation Sofie started. "As you know I have been going to the Methodist Church."

"Yeah, the free one."

"Yes . . . well, we are having special meetings with a guest speaker. Would you come with me?"

"No, absolutely not. That's not for me," he bluntly responded. Sofie drew a slow breath to regain her composure.

"Ernst, it would mean a lot to me if you would come for just one night," she said, coming at him from another angle. "That's all I ask. Just one night. I'll not trouble you after that. Will you do that?"

"But that stuff is only for old ladies. I don't want to be seen there."

Ernst and his aunt shared a mutual stubbornness. She tried to remain gracious. "I know a lot of ladies attend, but I'm so proud of you. Wouldn't you come just once for my sake?"

"All right. But just once and no more. Never again."

"Thank you, Ernst."

That evening Ernst advanced slowly toward the small meeting hall of the Methodist church, but walked ahead of his aunt so that no one would guess where he was going. He looked at the bold steeple on the beautiful Lutheran Church and thought of how contemptible it was to be going to the little Methodist church. The assurance that it was only a once-and-done deal helped.

Ernst and Sofie entered the back door. They were late, and the meeting had already begun. Ernst surveyed the group of about forty people and saw only five men. The tall woman greeting everyone at the door stunned the worshipers to silence when she bellowed like a pipe organ in

Ernst's direction, "Welcome, welcome!" The congregation turned in unison to gaze upon his reddening face.

Ernst was terrified when he noticed that the only available seats were up front. There was no way out. "Please, please come and be seated," said the lady, leading them to the very first row. Ernst walked down the aisle as though going to his execution, while his aunt wore a look of victory on her face. They sat down. Ernst slouched over in the pew, wishing he were invisible.

He was even more startled when the speaker was introduced. "Tonight, our guest speaker is Sister Maria from the Baltic State."

A woman! thought Ernst with indignation. *I came to a church full of old ladies only to hear a woman speak?* He thrust his finger into his collar to ease what felt like a noose tightening around his neck.

Then Sister Maria stood. She was short, stocky and looked angry enough to scare the devil himself. Ernst nearly laughed aloud when she stepped behind the pulpit and almost disappeared. It was as though a talking head were perched on the podium. Her chubby finger thrust into the air, punctuating her statements, and her strong voice rose and fell. Allowing no time for small talk, she got right to the point. As for Ernst, however, her words flowed without obstruction in one ear and out the other. Suddenly, all changed when she shot a word with cannon force directly at the lethargic lad: "Hypocrite! . . . you're a hypocrite!" she boomed, her finger pointing at Ernst, her eyes piercing his soul.

Ernst felt his defenses weaken when a voice deep within seemed to say, "She's right."

Sister Maria snarled on with holy boldness, "You are different at night when nobody can see you than you are in the daytime when everybody is watching."

Ernst tried to get angry, but couldn't. Just as he had heard nothing up until that word was spoken, so he heard nothing after it. The voice within latched onto the word "hypocrite" and condemned him more severely than Sister Maria. *How does she know about me?* he wondered. *Did my aunt talk to her? I must get out of here. I'll never be back. No more of this for me!*

The meeting ended. He and Aunt Sofie walked home. The sun's afterglow lingered on the horizon and the deep sky looked like a velvet cloth spread to display the brilliant stars. A crescent moon hung sharply on the sky's edge. The air was brisk and invigorating. But Ernst's heart was clogged with condemnation. It was that persistent inner voice. Was it his conscience . . . or God? He didn't know. Nor did he care. He was ensnared by the word "hypocrite."

Returning home, he went to his room, lit a cigarette and lay with one arm bent behind his head. His mind flooded with memories. *It's true*, he thought. *I do things in private that I would be ashamed to have people see. I say things that I would never want the village to know. I act friendly, but I'm full of hate. I act tough but feel afraid. I am two people. I am a hypocrite.*

The clock downstairs struck midnight, but Ernst was wide awake . . . fixated in thought. Scenes passed before his mind's eye. He thought of his days at the school and remembered how superior he had felt. *But it was an illusion*, he thought. *How can we be superior, then lose our country to inferior people?* His thoughts turned to the prison. *How can we consider ourselves civilized, then fight like animals over a*

piece of bread? What is so superior about the way my country-
men talked? And what is so special about me?

He heard the clock strike 1, then 2, then 3. Still, no sleep.
Is everyone like me? No, there's Robert. He's different. He gave
me bread when other men fought over theirs. He helped me when
others treated me like dirt. What does he have? What makes him
different? Then there's Mrs. Eisenman. Her husband is expected
to be good, since he's a pastor, but she didn't have to be good. Yet,
she cared for my feet. But I felt something deeper happening. She
put salve on my feet, which soothed my heart as well.

Ernst tossed and turned. One thought crowded the
next. His wall of self-protection could not keep out the
thoughts that danced like whirlwinds, nor could it resist
the inner voice that seemed to probe him throughout the
night. Conviction crawled over the wall and into his heart
like fog seeping over the bastion of a castle. It moved freely
into every inner room, leaving no place to hide. He fought
hard to keep his fortress strong and sturdy, but he was losing the battle. At long last, as he heard a rooster crowing,
he fell asleep, exhausted by the long night's war.

CHAPTER TEN

The Radical Choice

The mid-morning autumn air was cool as Ernst awakened; still, sweat beads glossed his chest. He opened his eyes and looked around the room. Although everything was the same, he felt as though he had wrestled with the devil all night. He had. But the war went beyond that. He had wrestled with himself also . . . and with God.

He went downstairs. Sofie was in her sewing room. "Ready for some breakfast?" she asked.

"Yes."

"I'll fix it now," she said as she gracefully moved toward the kitchen. She fanned the embers in the stove that were still glowing from the early morning breakfast she had prepared for her husband and placed new sticks on them. They snapped and crackled into flames. Ernst stared at them, wishing something would ignite in his heart to lift him out of the heaviness he felt. Then came the surprise.

"Aunt Sofie, I'm going back to the meeting with you tonight."

His aunt nearly dropped the kettle she was holding, but quickly recovered. "That will be nice, Ernst," she said with amazing control.

"But," said Ernst, lifting his forefinger to make his point sure, "we must be there on time. I want to sit near the back and not be paraded to the front."

"Certainly," Sofie responded, relieved that the terms were reasonable.

That evening the two walked through the church door. People milled about, warmly greeting each other. Ernst claimed a seat to the right side safely in the back, one he felt sure would offer protection from the big woman whose booming voice had embarrassed him the night before.

Soon the meeting started. Ernst listened with interest, wondering if that inner voice would trouble him again. At long last it was time for Sister Maria to speak. Her subject was the love and forgiveness of God. As she stepped behind the pulpit and peered over the top, Ernst didn't feel like laughing. In fact, he braced himself to see if he could fend off her words and forget about this religious talk.

Sister Maria lacked humor. Abruptly, she raised her arm, pointed to the ceiling and pontificated, "How can we doubt God's love? God sent His Son to the cross to die for our sins. God sent His Holy Spirit to draw us to Himself. That's the voice you sense within. It's God inviting you to His love and mercy. God loves you. God wants you, but you must decide whether or not you'll respond to that love. What a terrible thing it is to refuse God's love—a love that cost God His Son's life."

Ernst sat transfixed, listening to two voices—hers and that inner voice. Two messages coursed through his mind. As she preached, he recalled the people whom he had met, people who exhibited the changed life she was describing: Aunt Sofie . . . Robert . . . Elizabeth Eisenman. Their examples proved the truth of Sister Maria's words.

He lightened at the thought of being like them. *But can I be like them?* he wondered. *Is it possible?*

The meeting ended all too soon. Deep in thought, Ernst remained as people left. Then he saw Sister Maria coming toward him. He braced for trouble, but she plowed right through his wall of resistance, asking, "Would you like to pray?"

Unmoved, he returned her stare. He thought, *Lady, you don't know where I've been; what I've been through.* But the arguments in his mind seemed to weaken.

Tightening his lips he blurted, "I don't know *what* to pray."

"Just talk to the Lord as you would talk to anyone else. Tell him exactly what you're thinking."

Ernst had no problem with that. He was part of a civilization that had been duped once, but refused to let it happen again. This made the people blunt and matter-of-fact in attitudes and words. So Ernst bowed his head, closed his eyes and began: "If it is true what this woman says . . . if You are truly the same as I heard tonight, then I would like to give my whole life to be dedicated to You—only to You alone. I will hold nothing back from You."

He looked up, the expression on his face as candid as his prayer, but still feeling nothing. Sister Maria smiled for the first time, squeezed his shoulder and walked away. There he stood, alone.

"Aunt Sofie, I'd like to walk home by myself."

"Of course, Ernst. I'll see you there later."

Ernst walked out the door. The night was a carbon copy of the previous one, except that the moon was a slice larger. Looking up to the sky, he exclaimed, "I meant what I said, God," not knowing that God had already smashed the wall of his fortress. It had begun to fall, and the hate, bitterness and confusion were draining out. He didn't feel like a prisoner in his own body anymore. His heart felt lighter with each step. Soon an uncontainable joy was pouring into the crevices vacated by rage. He inhaled the night air more deeply than ever.

When he finally arrived home, he found his sister Hedwig visiting with Sofie. He burst out, "Tonight I became a child of God! I know I did."

"You fool! How can you know that?" Hedwig snapped back, storming out of the room. Ernst was amazed that her cynicism didn't dent his resolve. Sofie dabbed her eyes, however, choking back tears of joy.

That night, lying alone, Ernst thought . . . and he felt . . . and he thought . . . and he felt. He placed his hands on his chest, took a deep breath and exhaled to see if the change in him would depart. It didn't. He was a new person and he knew it. "Nothing could make me feel so clean, so new except You, Lord," he prayed.

I committed my whole being to the Fuehrer and he failed, Ernst thought. Then he said out loud, "God, I made a radical choice tonight to commit myself completely to You. I'm ready and willing to serve You in any way You choose." It was then that an awareness entered his heart. It wasn't audible or mystical, just a quiet, settled sense that he was not to be a teacher. Ernst felt an odd mingling of disappointment and peace as he let go of his dream. He had no idea what God wanted for his life, but he felt certain it was not to teach.

A startling thought then occurred to him. *What if I'm to be a pastor? Oh, no! Not one of those men who wears black suits during the week and black robes on Sunday.* He didn't know if he could bargain with God, but that was one thing he was sure he did not want to be. Ernst recoiled at the thought. Then, convicted, he yielded: "Lord, You can show me what it is You want me to do . . . where I'm to go . . . how I'm to serve."

As he drifted off, it was as though he slept on a cloud. He arose with a longing to tell his father what had happened. After breakfast he headed for his parents' home. He couldn't believe how freely his feet moved. Up the steps past the barn he bounded, opened the door and entered the kitchen like an evangelist on the attack. His unsuspecting dad was sitting at the large kitchen table enjoying breakfast, while his mother was standing at the stove. Ernst plopped down and looked Victor directly in the eyes.

"Dad, I must tell you what happened to me." Victor's spoon clanked against his cup as he stirred his coffee. Saying nothing, he nodded for Ernst to speak.

"Last night I became a child of God at the Methodist Church meeting. He is now my heavenly Father." The clanking spoon stopped. The last sound was his mother awkwardly adjusting the kettle on the stove. The silence was brittle.

Stunned by his son's shameless aggressiveness, Victor broke the silence and spoke: "We are a Christian family, aren't we? But we are not fanatics. I don't like a stubborn fanatic like you have become. You confess that you have a heavenly Father?" Ernst nodded affirmatively. "And you have a father on earth." Ernst nodded again. "Now, choose. Nobody has two fathers, only one. So you choose right now which one you want."

"You are my father, but I cannot deny my heavenly Father."

"OK, no more. So your Father is in heaven? Finished."

Ernstine put her hands to her face and lifted her head as though releasing a silent scream. The sword of Christ had just fallen between father and son.

Ernst leaned against the back of the chair. He couldn't believe what was happening within his heart. He had just been banished by his father, but he now felt a love for him greater than any he had ever known.

Undaunted in spirit, he rose from his chair and heard the most amazing words come from his lips: "I love you, Dad. I love you, Mom," and he left. Now he could only hope that his new Father would prove faithful and true. He felt sure that He would.

That night he prayed, *Father, You had to take me through some awful experiences to open my eyes to Your strength in salvation. I don't think I would have ever turned to You without the things I have seen. But now I need someone to help teach me Your way.*

God had heard his prayer before Ernst had even called.

CHAPTER ELEVEN

Cake and Commitment

"**E**rnst. Let's go! It's nearly 2 o'clock." It was time for the weekly Sunday afternoon soccer game. A fellow member was calling his team goalie from the front porch. Ernst was torn, however, because there was a Bible study being held at the same time.

"I think this will be my last game," Ernst confided as they walked to the field. "Next Sunday I will attend the meeting at the church."

Wrinkling his nose, his friend exclaimed, "Church! Are you crazy?" Then his voice took on a teasing tone, "Myrtha will be at the game today . . . like always."

"Myrtha is just a friend, and soccer is just a game. I made a commitment to God, so I must go to the meeting," Ernst replied.

The following Sunday Ernst showed up at the service. The sun streamed through the high windows. His body argued, *It's Sunday afternoon and time for fun. Let's go!* He heard his friends at the distant field starting the game, then looked around the room and noticed that the youngest man there was thirty-five. Ernst was seventeen. Still, he decided to stay, at least this once.

There was an appalling lull as each one "waited upon the Spirit" to lead someone to speak. This was followed by a boring discussion about how they should proceed. Ernst heard a distant cheer coming from the ball field. The sun beckoned him to activity, while these men seemed as motionless as undertakers officiating at a wake. Ernst passed from restlessness to disappointment and then to anger. At long last his high spirit and temper got the best of him. Standing up he bellowed a curse word that echoed throughout the cavernous meeting hall, sending the saints into shock. He didn't care. He lunged for the door. He was finished.

An old man standing at the door caught Ernst by the shoulders. "Ernst, it was not good what you just did, and you must never do it again. That's the last time. It's important that you stay. Please don't leave." Ernst took a few deep breaths and returned to his seat. While he was at level one of overcoming his hot temper, the men never did overcome their boring ways.

At the close of the session, Ernst saw a man he vaguely knew shuffling toward him, struggling to keep in step with his canes. Ernst recognized him as Willie Klein. Frostbite had claimed a large chunk of each foot while he was fighting in Russia during the war. "I want you to come home with me," he said.

"What for?" Ernst questioned, anxious from the boredom. He could still hear the crowd yelling at the soccer field.

"Cake. My wife made a cake, and we have fresh milk."

Ernst's rancor dissipated. They slowly walked a mile out of the village to Willie's little farm.

"Clara, this is Ernst Vatter. He is a new believer. I asked him to join us for a piece of cake."

"Hello, Ernst. Welcome to our home. Please sit over here at the table." Ernst didn't need to be directed twice. Soon the first piece of cake was in front of him.

"Ernst," began Willie, "I want to be your friend and help you grow spiritually. Would you like that?"

"OK," somehow slipped from between his stuffed cheeks.

"Ernst, there are many people who think they are Christians because they are members of a church, and even attend it at times. But Jesus Christ calls every believer to far more than that. He calls us to total commitment. The Savior made a total commitment to us. He has every right to expect a total commitment in return."

"I agree," replied Ernst finishing his cake. "What you are saying is what is burning in me. I made a commitment the other night to fully dedicate myself to God, but I don't know what to do now."

"First, Ernst, you must keep yourself from people who would pull you away from your commitment. As hard as it is to sit through the boring meetings at church while your friends are playing soccer, it is there that you will learn the principles of growth."

Ernst stared long and hard at Willie, then responded, "I feel like I'm trapped between friends who tempt and Christians who bore." Clara eased his agony by plunking another piece of cake before him. He liked Willie because he understood the fire burning within his heart for God. He liked Clara because she made a delicious cake. "At least I can have the two of you to lean on, can't I?"

"Certainly," came a harmonious duet.

"Tell me more, then, about what it means to be committed to God."

"There are two things I want you to know," Willie began. "They are so important that I will repeat them many times. First, if you are going to be a Christian, then be a wholehearted one—committed 100 percent. Otherwise, don't do it, just drop it. Decide now to pay any price necessary to follow Jesus Christ. Hold nothing back. God will lead your life.

"Second, whatever crosses your life's path will always be something that the Lord has either caused or allowed in order to fulfill His purpose for you. Remember that as long as you live."

The moment was sacred to Ernst. He felt that Willie was a very special man whom God was using to lay an important foundation. After another piece of cake he headed for home. Lighting a cigarette, he walked and prayed.

The following week Willie's words were put to the test. "There's a letter for you from the government," said Sofie.

Ernst picked it up from the table, tore it open and began to read: *Dear Mr. Vatter, The government is opening a new school. According to our records you were issued a pair of government shoes. Please return those shoes immediately. They are government property.*

It was winter; sending the shoes back would leave him with only a pair of sandals. Sofie took the letter and read it. "No!" she shouted. "You will not send those shoes back. This is a different government, and they do *not* have the right to ask for your shoes."

"It's true what they say. They're *not* my shoes. As a Christian, I must send them back."

"I am going to get Pastor Schule. He will talk sense into your head." Sofie stormed out of the house and returned thirty minutes later with Pastor Ernst Schule in tow.

"Ernst," said the pastor, "it would not be violating anything for you to keep the shoes."

Ernst's German bluntness and Christian commitment entered the same yoke as he said, "Pastor Schule, it's nice to have your help. But I don't tell you what you should preach, so please don't tell me what I should do."

The pastor blushed, rose to his feet and politely said, "All right. Good-bye," and left.

The next day, while Sofie was shopping, Ernst seized the opportunity to wrap the shoes and take them to the post office. Walking home he thought, *Now it's finished. It's final. Aunt Sofie can get as excited as she wants, but it can't be changed.* Then he prayed aloud, "Lord, You can give me some shoes. If it's Your will, it's no problem for You to give me a pair of shoes."

The next month was solemn around the house. Sofie staunchly held her ground, sure she was right. Then, several weeks later, a mysterious package arrived addressed to Ernst. He opened it to find the same shoes he had returned to the government. A note was included that read: *Dear Mr. Vatter, You were the only one in the whole country who returned his shoes. We do not believe it makes sense to keep only one pair, so you may keep them.*

Ernst looked up with the same victorious grin on his face that his aunt had worn when he first walked down the aisle of the little Methodist Church. "Now I have both shiny shoes and a clear conscience." Fresh in his thoughts were Willie's words that everything that comes into one's pathway is from the Lord. He had taken a risk in his first act of commitment, and God had honored him.

He regularly visited Willie's home to eat cake, enjoy conversation and learn about commitment. Willie and Clara made an unbeatable team. One filled Ernst's heart, the other his stomach.

"Willie," he said one night with great concern, "I wrote a letter to two girls I have dated telling them that I was ending all relationship with them in order to devote all of my attention to the Lord."

"Wonderful. I'm proud of you."

"It has caused a problem. One accepted my explanation, although she joins my other friends in making fun of me. The second, Myrtha, wrote that if I stop seeing her she will kill herself."

"Nonsense!" Willie shot back. "She won't kill herself. That's the tempter trying to turn you away. Clean the slate as you desire, and stay fully committed to God. He will work it out."

"Then that's what I'll do. But, Willie, I'm having problems with one more thing. An elderly man came to me the other night, pointed at this curly hair I inherited from my mother and said, 'I believe you are a Christian, but you can't be born again.' Surprised, I asked why. He responded, 'Because people with curly hair are always selfish.' I got really angry, but he still persisted in saying, 'If you were truly born again the Lord would have straightened your hair.' "

Willie let out an unusual roar of laughter. "Many Christians have silly ideas that you must ignore. Sadly, you'll rarely change them, so don't waste time trying. And don't waste energy getting angry."

Relieved, Ernst ran his fingers through his hair, again resting secure in his salvation.

"The time has come, Ernst, for me to teach you some important things," Willie continued. "First, the key to understanding biblical truth is balance. Any truth carried one step too far becomes a non-truth and does damage. You can only understand the Bible by balancing one truth against the other. Second, always remember that God must strip us of all strength in order to show us His. And third, every believer must walk the path of faith, believing God to lead him, though He leaves no footprints. You must walk by faith, not sight. It's one thing to sit at my table where we talk about faith and commitment, but the time is soon coming for you to walk the path alone."

His words loomed as a harbinger of days to come.

CHAPTER TWELVE

A Path Without Footprints

E arly in 1946 the time came for Ernst to walk a difficult path of faith. A letter arrived, inviting him to
study at the school he had attended in Esslingen,
which was now under a different government and in a new
location. It would open in Saulgau that September. With
no other options, the young eaglet was dropped from his
nest to spread his wings.

His time with Willie had drawn to a close. For the time
being, it would be no one but God and Ernst, alone.

Shortly after arriving at Saulgau, Ernst went for a long
walk. A cigarette dangled from his lips as he walked at a
slow pace, head down, disturbed. *How can I be committed to
Christ and still be so bound to cigarettes?* he wondered. The
enjoyment of smoking was gone. It had become a bondage.
At long last he sat down on a bench by a cemetery wall, an
appropriate setting for the prayer that he lifted.

*Lord, I told You that I would hold nothing back from You, but I
can't get rid of this habit of smoking. I am bound by it. Lord, Willie
taught me that I died on the cross with You, and that through Your
life I should be free in every way. Now, I am asking You to set me
free so that I can serve You more fully. I don't have the strength to
stop smoking. I'm asking You for Your strength.* He rose to his
feet, took the pack of cigarettes from his pocket and tossed

them into the cemetery as hard as he could. One part of him wanted to run after them, but the other part refused. There were weeks of struggle to follow, but the slave master of ciga-rette addiction lost its grip and died at the cemetery that day.

Ernst's tender faith had seen God provide shoes, protect him from Myrtha's threat of suicide and, now, grant strength to overcome smoking. He was in the early stages of passing by faith from strength to strength. But a new pressure was upon him, one that did not exist when he previously at-tended the government school as a nonbeliever. At that time he had been like all the others: arrogant, cynical and self-directed. This time he was changed. His identity was found in Christ as much as in his own name. But when he read his Bible and prayed in the dorm, mockery and laughter filled the halls. He was rejected by his peers.

"Look at this. Ernst is religious. He's a Jesus boy!" Taunts were followed by wild laughter. The battle for self-identity was on. With whom would he align himself for ac-ceptance, his peers or God? The professors were not on his side, since they were steeped in German rationalism and self-determination.

One afternoon Ernst sat under a tree praying. *Lord, I saw men laugh at Robert in the prison camp, and some villagers scoff at Willie's commitment. I know that all of Your followers in the Bible faced rejection too. Still, I feel a war within my heart. It's hard to be rejected by my friends.*

The taunts continued, but now they drove him toward God rather than away. To ease the pressure he faced in the dormitory, Ernst read his Bible under the blankets at night and prayed when alone. The mockery may have been part of what caused him to lose interest in teaching. He found himself praying, *God, I am not at home here. Are You leading me to a different path? I will stay here until You make Your will clear.*

The autumn leaves had fallen and blown away. The air grew frigid, and signs of Christmas appeared. Ernst returned to Goenningen for a weekend, and while there he went to a bookstore. Emma, the clerk, was a large woman with a round face, a strong voice and an overpowering personality. She had heard of Ernst's radical conversion. Her words to Ernst sounded like a Macedonian call.

"Ernst, you should go to Liebenzell."

"Liebenzell? Isn't that the small village in the Black Forest?"

"Yes, but it's more than that. Liebenzell is a mission."

"What's a mission?"

"It's an institution where young people are educated in the Bible, then sent to places, such as Africa. That's where you should go," she declared as finally as a judge's gavel.

"Well, that seems like a good idea. Could you look for application papers? If it's God's will, then they will accept me. If not, then that's OK too."

Emma rolled into action and, within weeks, Ernst had the papers completed and returned to the mission. After sending the application he prayed, "Lord, if it's Your will, I will go. If not, then have them turn me down."

When Ernst returned home from Saulgau for a weekend break in the spring of 1947, a letter from the Liebenzell Mission awaited him. He tore open the envelope and read: *Dear Mr. Vatter, We welcome you as a new student at Liebenzell. You will start on September 1, 1947.*

Typical of German communication, it was brief and to the point. So was Ernst's response. "OK, Lord, I will go." He then returned to Saulgau to finish the spring semester.

While Ernst was at home that summer, word spread of his intention to go to Liebenzell in order to study for the ministry. It spread all the way to Aunt Hedwig, one of his father's sisters, who by marrying Baron Von Crafft had become the Baroness Von Truchsess. The baron had been wealthy enough to have his own self-appointed pastor, who would preach in the village church where they had their own special box just opposite the pulpit.

Now widowed, Aunt Hedwig continued her aristocratic lifestyle. She lived in a castle 130 miles away, in the northern part of the state of Bavaria. The proud castle stood heavily planted near the village of Wetzhausen, not far from the city of Schweinfurt. To learn that her nephew was about to forfeit the privilege and prestige of being a minister in the Protestant church caused her to gasp. Ernst was summoned to the castle.

"My dear Ernst," began his aunt, "do you know what you are doing?" Her head was raised as though she was attempting to transcend a noxious odor. "This Liebenzell . . . I have never heard of it."

"Well, I have prayed about it, and that is where the Lord is leading me."

Hedwig lowered her dignity to sound sympathetic. "Don't tell me that. Oh, Ernst, you have such potential, and I will be able to help you. I will pay for everything if you will study theology in a reputable seminary to become a state church minister."

"Never!" he said emphatically.

"I will give you additional money," she said in an imploring manner.

"Keep it. I am going to Liebenzell because the Lord showed me to go this way."

"Please, Ernst, don't make this mistake." Hedwig didn't realize she was talking to a young man who had passed through an unjust and horrible imprisonment, faced his father's rejection of his faith, cut all friendships that would hinder his walk with God and overcome ridicule at school. He was young in years only, not experience.

"I am going to Liebenzell. God will take care of me. Thank you for your interest, Aunt Hedwig, but it is settled."

Ernst departed. The castle of opportunity diminished behind him, while the path of divine direction stretched before him. The first offered comfort, the latter demanded commitment. Determined, Ernst put one foot before the other, not looking for God's footprints, just His hand.

CHAPTER THIRTEEN

Mountain of Fire

"Willie, what do you think about the Liebenzell Mission?" inquired Ernst while gulping down some cake.

"I don't know much about it. What have you learned?"

Ernst's eyes brightened with excitement. "Rev. Heinrich Coerper was inspired by Hudson Taylor to begin a German branch of the China Inland Mission in Hamburg on November 13, 1899."

"That's a northern seaport. How did the mission end up in Bad Liebenzell?" asked Clara.

"Prayer! This is where it gets very exciting. It happened as a result of prayer. A deaconess named Sister Lina Stahl, who had been with the Stuttgart deaconate, was running a guest home down in the valley in the village of Liebenzell. For years she had been looking at the mountain from her guest home, praying that the Lord would make it like a volcano, spewing the flames of the gospel around the world."

"That sounds like a prayer inspired by God's Spirit," said Willie.

"Yes, I agree. And, just like her name 'Stahl' implied, she remained as strong as steel and steadfast in her prayer.

"Then one day she learned that the city of Hamburg was going to put a road right through the building that housed the mission there, and that they had to move by April 4, 1902. So she prayed that God would lead the mission to Bad Liebenzell. She wrote to Rev. Coerper on January 25, 1902, inviting him to come south to see the mountain for himself. He was not excited about the invitation, since there were other offers, but he finally responded to her persistence. Visiting Bad Liebenzell with his wife, he was both impressed and discouraged—impressed by the potential and discouraged by the rent."

By now, Willie, who loved to trust God for impossible things, had slid to the edge of his chair. Allowing his coffee to get cold he asked, "How did the mission afford such a large place?"

Ernst, who had mastered the skill of handling cake and conversation at the same time, continued. "On February 2, Hilda Von Diest, the wealthy wife of a general and friend to Sister Lina, offered to assist with the rent, making the mountain no more costly to the mission than the place they had in Hamburg. They moved the mission to Liebenzell on April 5, 1902. Then in 1903, the owner wanted to sell the mountain, but the price was far beyond the mission's resources."

Willie grinned, anticipating divine intervention.

"That's when God answered Sister Stahl's prayer more fully. Mrs. Diest bought the mountain and gave it to the mission with only one stipulation: They could use the mountain so long as they had a school that was equipping young people to take the gospel around the world. Should they stop doing that, they would forfeit the mountain. When China closed to missions, the vision for the mountain expanded to the entire world. So on July 6, 1906, the name was changed to Liebenzell Mission, in partnership with the China Inland Mission."

Then, a flash of historical insight lit the room when Ernst said, "Just think, Hitler stood on his mountain at Berchtesgaden dreaming of how he was going to change the world. His plans are now dust. Sister Stahl prayed to God for the fire of His Spirit to erupt and send forth from that mountain trained missionaries to change eternity. And servants have been going like firebrands around the world ever since."

"What a contrast," Clara added, as she refilled their coffee cups. "Man's best plans come to nothing, but God's purposes stand forever."

"That's what I want for my life," said Ernst. "I want to fulfill the will of God, and you two have helped me more than anyone else to learn how to do that."

"There's a fire burning in you, Ernst," said Willie. "That fire will soon touch the fire on the mount. I believe God has big plans for you."

For Ernst, the previous summer had been long, boring and lacking in promise. This summer was different. The fire in his heart raged more each day as he read his Bible, prayed and dreamed of serving God somewhere around the world. It was late August when he departed Goenningen for the fourth time. This was the first time, however, that he left with a sense of eternal destiny.

"Willie, I came to say good-bye to you and Clara. Thank you, Clara, for all of the cake. You are a wonderful cook. And thank you, Willie, for your encouragement."

Willie's eyes were misty. "Clara and I will be praying that you will live your entire life fully committed to the Lord. I hope you'll keep in touch."

Then Ernst went to see his parents. His father was willing to have him visit in his home, but he would never be seen on the streets with the son who possessed such a zeal for God. Bounding up the steps to the kitchen Ernst shouted, "Good morning, Mom. Good morning, Dad. I'm leaving for Liebenzell. I came to say good-bye."

Victor, drinking coffee at the kitchen table, grunted in such a way as to appear human yet show no sign of agreement. Ernstine's eyes glistened as she smiled, her sparkly spirit brightening the room.

"Take care, Ernst. We will be thinking about you. Please write . . ."

The words were barely out of her mouth before the impetuous Ernst was gone.

He next ran to the post office to say farewell to his uncle, who was characteristically quiet. Then he darted to his home to grab his bag of clothes and say a quick good-bye to Aunt Sofie. They embraced, and she shoved a sandwich in his pocket as he charged out the door for the bus. From the bus, he changed to the train at Reutlingen, then continued seventy-five miles northwest to the edge of the Black Forest and the town of Bad Liebenzell.

Ernst was accustomed to the dramatic mountains and hills of southwest Germany, so he gave little thought to the topography as the train stopped at the convergence of mountains where Bad Liebenzell was nestled in the valley. The village flared up the hem of the surrounding hills. Hot mineral springs flowed in the valley, and a castle perched high on a hill. Because of the springs, the village was called Bad (meaning bath) Liebenzell.

Getting off the train, Ernst walked toward the mission compound, which was housed on thirty acres of land sloping up the south side of the town. The dormitory was a mammoth building jutting high out of the hillside. Perhaps best described as a European ski lodge, Rev. Coerper had designed it to combine beauty, art, solidity and functionality.

Following registration, Ernst dumped his clothes into a drawer and walked to the top of the mountain. There he prayed: *Lord, this is the place where You led Sister Lina to pray for a great moving of Your Spirit's fire. I will do all in my power to prepare. I ask You for Your help, and I pray that You will send me as another flaming tongue from this mountain to some place in the world. I want to spread to others this powerful gospel that has transformed me.*

Ernst tipped his head back to look at the evening sky. Birds flew across the wispy pink clouds that were strewn about as though tossed by a sower. He couldn't help but look back at the path from which he had come. It was only a little more than two years ago that he had been choking on the horrid odors in the German tank garage and, even worse, suffocating in his own hatred. It had been just two brief years since his conversion to Christ, followed by a radical choice to wholeheartedly follow Him. As recently as six months earlier he was the main focus of mockery at the government school at Saulgau. Now, he sat on top of God's fire mountain, looking at an open sky, inhaling fresh air and seeing an unhindered horizon of opportunity before him. All he could do was thank the Lord over and over again.

That night he prayed a specific prayer: *Lord, some people seem to have Your message in their mind but not Your fire in their heart. I want to be one who has both the message and the fire. On the night I met You, I promised that I would hold nothing back from You. But still I find my bitterness toward the French to be a stumbling block. It rises up like an unannounced firestorm in my heart in the middle of the night. I try to forget it but I cannot. I'm asking You to show me how to be free so that my spirit may be clean and wholly committed to You.*

It wouldn't be long until his answer began to unfold.

CHAPTER FOURTEEN

The Power of Forgiveness

Ernst plunged into his studies at the mission school in Bad Liebenzell with abandon. The truths challenged his mind while the Spirit inflamed his heart. He resolved to take both facts and fire to the world.

Ernst bore his mother's buoyant temperament, which found laughter as natural as breathing. One morning he entered the chapel laughing with his friends, but sobered when he saw a few stiff German eyebrows arching high. While Ernst admired these pietistic professors, he thought, *Surely God will allow me to keep my mother's gift of humor.*

That morning's speaker was Pastor Bitterhof, the dean of students and professor of Greek. His talk held Ernst's attention.

"Around 1600," he began, "a man in Holland named Rubens was accused of adultery. He was sentenced to death, which was the law in that day. His wife could not stand the gossip and humiliation that flooded upon her, so she fled to Siegen, Germany.

"In time she got a letter from her imprisoned husband pleading for forgiveness. She wrote back assuring him that she had already forgiven him—for all time! She wrote that she and the children prayed for him every night, knowing of the terrible suffering he faced. She added that in light of Jesus' suffering, her suffering from his unfaithfulness was a small matter to forgive.

"At midnight, prior to the day of his execution, her letter fell into the hands of the judges in Holland. They were so moved by it that they pardoned the man, who immediately moved to Siegen where he and his wife resumed their marriage and eventually had another son. This son became one of the most famous painters in all the world. Today a Rubens painting can sell for $1 million to $5 million. So, you see, this woman's forgiveness not only spared her husband's life, but gave a gift of art to the world.

"The key thing I want you to remember is that forgiveness can bring a great gift to you and to the whole world."

Ernst felt slain by the words. How could he take the gospel to the world if he still held bitterness toward the French? He knew he had to surrender it, but did not know how. Every time he tried to forget the past, a voice inside reminded him of the way he had been violated.

After chapel, Ernst approached the speaker. "Pastor Bitterhof, I'm having a terrible time coping with forgiveness. May I speak with you?"

"Of course," the pastor replied. "Come to my home tonight at 7 o'clock."

That evening Ernst knocked on the pastor's door and was greeted by Mrs. Bitterhof, who led him into the living room. Pastor Bitterhof was still wearing a suit and sat cross-legged in a large overstuffed chair. The knuckles of his left hand were folded under his chin with the forefinger pointing to his cheekbone. *A scholarly pose*, thought Ernst. The gold chain of his pocket watch dipped across the front of his vest and a monocle dangled from his neck. Ernst took special note of everything, assuming that this is how he would look someday when he became a scholar.

"It's wonderful to see you, Ernst. Please be seated and tell me what's on your mind."

Ernst sat down and began, conscious of the need to enunciate every word. "The story you told in chapel today moved me deeply. There are some things that happened in my past that I can't forgive. I try, but it's too hard. The memories won't stop stirring bitterness."

"Do you mind telling me what happened?"

"After the war, French soldiers mistook me for my older brother and took me to a prison camp. They treated us worse than dogs. We were starved and kept in filth. They laughed as they degraded and humiliated all of us. Sometimes at night I can still hear the sound of their voices, even see their faces, and I crave revenge. Although this happened two-and-a-half years ago, it burns in me to this day."

With compassion and understanding, Pastor Bitterhof said, "Ernst, forgiveness of great offenses often takes time; it's a process. In Matthew 18:22, Jesus told us to forgive seventy times seven. Perhaps it's this process that he had in mind when he said that. In other words, you may have to work through forgiveness that many times before the heart quiets into peace. It will take time, but don't give up."

"It helps me to know that I'm not responsible for the feelings that come back," Ernst replied.

"No, you're not responsible. You have reasons for the way you feel, but not rights. You have reason to be a bitter, angry man and to want revenge. But only God has the right to inflict judgment, so the beginning of forgiveness is to turn over your reasons and rights to God. I believe that's what kept Jesus free of bitterness. He kept laying His reasons and rights down before God."

"That's not easy to do," said Ernst quietly.

"It's hard because we want to be sure justice is served. We're afraid that forgiveness will let an enemy off the hook. Not so. Forgiveness hands an enemy to God as the judge. If an enemy does not make things right with us, then God will deal with that person at the proper time. Further, we don't forgive because we fear God won't beat up our enemies as badly as we desire."

"That's true," Ernst laughed, feeling as though Pastor Bitterhof was looking into his very soul. "It's like there are two fires inside of me. The fire of the Spirit cleanses me, while the fire of these memories turns my heart to burnt bitter ashes. You're saying that I may have to fight between the two fires seventy times seven before forgiveness extinguishes the fire of bitterness?"

"Yes, that's a good way to put it. Now, Ernst, I must say something extremely important. If you do not fight to win by the power of forgiveness, then you will hand the French soldiers the key to your soul. You'll empower them to stand as guards, keeping you a prisoner of bitterness for the rest of your life. Only forgiveness will break their power."

"I see. That's a frightening thought."

Professor Bitterhof continued. "I've learned in life that God often tests our spiritual growth by seeing if we will learn to love the thing we hate. I suspect that someday you may be called to serve the French."

Ernst stared at the floor, wondering if he would ever be able to do that. He had promised to hold nothing back from God, but to execute his bitterness with the strong arm of forgiveness seemed impossible. It was one thing to theorize about loving and forgiving the French, but the idea of having his commitment tested with service nearly made him gag.

"It's going to take a lot of time and work to forgive them, Pastor Bitterhof," Ernst said finally.

"My wife and I will pray for you."

Ernst returned to his dorm room with mixed emotions: excitement to think that he could extinguish the destructive fire of bitterness, and fear that he may someday be called to serve his enemies.

CHAPTER FIFTEEN

The Refiner's Fire

"Your commitment will be tested from every side," Willie had once said. Never could Ernst imagine that this would include a refining firestorm striking the school itself. The founder of the mission, Pastor Heinrich Coerper, had been replaced as mission director by Pastor Buddeberg on January 1, 1934. Buddeberg served for twelve years and resigned in the spring of 1946. In the fall of the year the board installed a Lutheran pastor named Gerhard Moeller as the third director of the mission.

Pastor Moeller took the school by storm with his great sermons on missions. Slowly, however, a cloud of controversy formed over the mission when it became clear that he wanted to move the school away from the faith tradition of Hudson Taylor. His goal was to change the global vision to send out more ecumenically minded missionaries. The wrongfulness was that he had accepted the position with this hidden agenda in mind. Moeller was a most gracious man, which made his plot hard to detect. His kindness was in stark contrast to the less pleasant disposition of many other leaders in the school, which greatly enhanced his cause.

His next move was to bring a new professor, Dr. Loeser, onto the faculty—one whose views collided with the doctrinal views of Liebenzell. The liberalism that was strangling the life out of the Great Reformation attempted to wrap its fingers around the Liebenzell students when Professor Loeser announced, "We will not consider the first eleven chapters of Genesis, since they merely contain myth." Word that a theological death angel had stepped on campus raced to the board. In an emergency meeting the board told Moeller that Loeser had to go. Moeller's response was that if one was thrown out, the other would leave too. The board's answer was simple: Both must go.

The student body was heartsick at the news. The men seemed so respectable that it was hard to believe they could be doing something unethical. Both Moeller and Loeser spoke to classes and met with students one-on-one, encouraging them to leave with them. Moeller assured all who would listen, "If you come with me, I will talk to the Bishop and assure you positions as pastors in the state church."

Ernst had said no to human promises at his aunt's castle. Now he was faced with the same test, only this time by a seemingly sweet-spirited professor on the "mount of fire." This test of commitment was far more subtle. One by one all of Ernst's classmates bit the lure and packed to leave. Ernst stood alone in his choice; soon he would be the only student remaining in his class.

One day, Moeller stopped Ernst as he walked across the campus. "Ernst, you are a good student with a fine personality and strong commitment to the Lord. This is no place for you. Come with me."

"I will pray about it."

Feeling abandoned and empty, Ernst went to the top of the mountain. His entire class was following the Pied Piper of opportunity, and he was left behind. *Are they right?* he wondered. *Am I a hard-headed fool? Will I end up with nothing? Will I be the laughingstock of the religious world?* He lifted his burdened thoughts to the Lord.

Lord, this is most confusing. All my classmates are leaving with Dr. Moeller, but I feel I cannot leave. If You are the One who led me here, then only You have the right to lead me away. So, until I hear otherwise from You, I will stay!

Loneliness became his closest friend. The dorm creaked from the wind but not from footsteps. Ernst's class now consisted of two people—a professor and him. At times he felt haunted by an inner mockery saying, *You fool! When will you ever learn? You are going to lose.*

"No!" he said one day out loud, "you will be quiet. I am not called to be a pastor. It was the Lord who led me here, and He has not led me away. The Lord can raise me up or cast me down. That is His right. My job is to obey. Call it stubbornness . . . call it commitment, I will stay." And so he did. The voice fell silent.

As Ernst remained steadfast in his commitment to God's leading, so he fully expected to see God remain faithful in His commitment to him. A deep pact began to form between Ernst and God: faith obedience by one and faithful leadership by the other.

His conviction that God led him to the Liebenzell Mission was enhanced by an experience he had during the next fall semester. *Lord,* Ernst prayed one night, *I need a sweater in order to endure the cold winter. Everyone is still recovering from the war, and no one can afford one. It's no problem for You to provide*

*a sweater; after all, You had the new government return my good
shoes. So, I ask You for it in Jesus' name.*

Ernst was not vague in his request; he told the Lord the
exact sweater he wanted. Weeks later a package arrived
for him. The postmark was illegible. He opened it to discover the *very* sweater he had requested. *I can't read who
sent it, Lord, so I have only You to thank. I will have to thank
this person in heaven. I take this as evidence that I made the
right decision to stay here.*

Then, the refining fire turned on Ernst. One day he was
having a disagreement with a lower-classman over a Scripture text, which led to a violent blowup. He was so enraged over his friend's thickheadedness that he nearly
cursed. His lips quivered as he stormed away.

Ernst's anger had erupted many times before. A large part
of the wall surrounding his heart had yet to be collapsed, and
behind it was a young man still learning the way of faith over
a good fight. He had no patience for slow-moving, dull
Christians. The fact that they might have a rightful view-
point had never crossed into his radar path. He was deeply
troubled, however, knowing that he had to change; otherwise, his explosive temper could render him unfit for service.

Heavy in heart he again ascended the "mount of fire" to
pray. His prayer started quietly, but soon took on its own
rage: "Lord, I have a real problem with anger, and I can't
do much about it. I don't want it. I know it is dangerous.
But I can't stop it. SO WHY DON'T YOU STOP IT!
WHERE ARE YOU? WHY DON'T YOU HELP ME? . . ."

Sweat dripped. Ernst wiped his brow, shocked that he
had just ranted at God. He wasn't sure if he was shaking
from the sudden rush of adrenaline or the fact that he had

survived such an insolent act. But there he stood, alone, disgusted with himself.

He was still breathing heavily when he heard footsteps drawing near. Trying to compose himself, he saw elderly Mr. Hauser, a lay leader in the fellowship group that supported the mission.

"How are you, Ernst? What are you doing up here?"

Ernst shrugged, not wanting to admit what had happened.

Mr. Hauser thrust a question straight at Ernst. "What's wrong? Tell me what your problem is."

"I blew up again. I was praying about my hot temper, and then I stormed at God. There's no hope."

"You're fighting the wrong way. There is no victory when you act like that. Blowing up comes from the anger that is deep within your heart. Unlike a volcano, for you blowing up doesn't ease the pressure. It only builds greater pressure. It's futile to say 'I don't want to blow up anymore.' Rather, you must learn to apply Romans 6 to your life. You have died with Christ on the cross to the power of sin. Therefore, you are free to live in the resurrection power of Jesus Christ."

Ernst looked quizzically at the older man. Mr. Hauser smiled and continued.

"OK, you see, it works this way. The outburst starts in the stomach. You try to hold it down but slowly it builds and rises until it is right at your throat. That's the last stop before it comes out. Instead of trying to push it back down yourself, simply pray, 'Lord, I thank You that I don't need to react by blowing up any more. I died with You on the cross. Now, I am free to react in the strength of Your resurrection power.' "

"But if I no longer have anger and explode, how can I get anything done?"

"Instead of acting in your own strength, a far greater power begins to work within you."

"What's that?"

"The fruit of the Holy Spirit: love, joy, peace, longsuffering, gentleness, meekness, kindness, faithfulness, self-control."

Ernst took a deep breath. The insight was flushing out improper belief. More pieces of the wall around his heart cracked, crumbled and fell away. Then it dawned on him that he had used the same approach—relying on Christ's strength—to overcome smoking. That day he began to apply it to his hot temper. Then he realized that this truth could be applied to every area of life. While he would face repeated battles with his temper, at least he knew how to fight it—with the victory established by Christ on the cross.

Ernst felt relief to know that the gospel not only delivered him from an eventual hell, but also daily from the controlling hell within his heart—literally, to deliver him from *himself*. He descended the hill, his heart light, hardly able to wait for the first opportunity to try this approach.

He didn't have to wait long. A few hours later, Robert Mohr, an older, well-respected student, approached him. Though Robert had been shot in the head during the war, his mind was not affected.

"Ernst, I want to talk with you," he said. "I have noticed that you are spending one hour in prayer every morning. It can be a good thing to pray that much, but I don't think you have the right motives. To me you seem to be competitive, trying to be better than your underclassmen. Perhaps you are attempting to get God to use you more than anyone else."

There was instant fire in Ernst's stomach that quickly raged up his throat. But before it could spew out, Ernst remembered, *You don't need anger. You can respond in the fruit of the Spirit.*

"Robert," he replied, "what you have said angers me, but that is because I think you are right. I am highly competitive and need to examine my motives. I thank you for your observation."

He walked away feeling liberated. He had left his anger on the cross with Christ. Later, he walked past Robert's room. The door was ajar, and he saw Robert kneeling and holding his head. He opened the door slightly and spoke.

"Robert? Are you all right?"

Robert looked up at Ernst. White finger marks were imprinted upon his reddened forehead. "I'm praying, Ernst."

"Oh, brother, I'm sorry to disturb you."

"No, it's OK. Let me explain. I have splitting headaches every day from the bullet. The only way to endure the pain is to thank the Lord that He chose to let me get shot in order to fulfill His purposes in my life. If I didn't praise and thank Him, I'd never be able to stand the pain."

"You have taught me much today about both of us. Thank you," Ernst said, then departed.

That night he lay alone in his room thinking of Willie's words, *Your commitment will be tested from every side.* He said aloud, "It's true, Lord. Pressures come from both within and without to turn me away from following You. So where do we go from here?"

Abruptly, a new thought struck him: It was time to consider a wife. "I'm sure You have some thoughts about that too, Lord. We'll talk about it tomorrow." Then he rolled over and fell asleep.

CHAPTER SIXTEEN

The Grumpy Groomsman

The window was opened wide through the night. The next morning Ernst awakened with a sneeze. His head was clogged with the rich scent of blossoms filling the air. He rolled onto his back and looked to the horizon where the sun was slicing open a new day. The impact upon the young man was predictable. *It would be nice to wake up with a wife beside me*, he thought.

At lunch a fellow student opened the subject of marriage. "Ernst, you'll graduate in a year. I know you want to go to the mission field, but the mission will expect you to get married first. I hope you have someone in mind." That evening Ernst went to the mountaintop to pray about it.

"Lord, You know that I need a wife. I want You to choose her, otherwise I will not marry. I will not take just any wife, however. In order for her to be a helper, she must be able to do things that I can't do, so I have five conditions for a wife: She must be pretty; after all, I have to look at her for a long time. She must know Latin because I know only Greek. She must play the piano or organ because I have no musical gift. She must be able to conduct a choir. And she must be willing to stay with me through both good and bad times. I know, Lord, that You can give me the right wife. So, I look to You. Amen."

Ernst's prayer was exceedingly serious. He wanted a *real* woman . . . a woman of God. So Ernst lifted that prayer to God each evening.

Then in 1949 he received a letter from his sister, which read: *Dear Ernst, I am going to marry and would like you to be a groomsman.*

Ernst was as shocked at his response as was his sister. But fearing that walking with a girl in a public setting could ruin his testimony, he replied: *Dear Hedwig, no, I will not be a groomsman at your wedding. I don't want to walk with a woman I don't know. Sorry.*

His sister plowed right into his fears: *Dear Ernst, you are my brother, and I insist that you do it.*

Wham! She was as feisty as he. He turned to a professor for advice and got hit from the other side. "You go! You have only one sister. But don't be a dog that doesn't bark. Open your eyes and mouth to the opportunity and be a real testimony for Christ in front of the other people."

That was that. Ernst accepted, not knowing that this was the divine hand moving him along the path of destiny.

The wedding day arrived, and Ernst's moment to be a bold witness came at the reception dinner. Hedwig had asked him to say a few words to the guests. His knees felt as weak as the groom's. Having grown up in a small village where gossip runs deep and opinions run high, he was terrified to get on a platform before the people who knew him—they would be judging everything about him. Feeling the weight of their eyes, he began to speak. His comments were brief but brilliant:

"Before Jesus began his ministry, he appeared as a guest at a wedding in Cana, just seven miles from his hometown of Nazareth. But even as a guest, his involvement made everything different: Tasteless water became flavorful; colorless water became deep red. If Jesus makes that kind of an impact as a guest, imagine what he can do as the Lord of the house and your life."

Sitting among the family and friends was Sigrid, the younger sister of Erika, the bride's attendant. Sigrid was shy and quiet. Her round face and full brown eyes gave her a natural and wholesome beauty. She listened to Ernst with rapt attention, noticing his strong eyes and square jaw, and was especially struck by learning of his intention to be a missionary.

"Come sit over here, Sigrid," said Erika as she left Ernst's side. With lamb-like innocence Sigrid sat down. Ernst greeted her, then looked at her . . . and looked at her . . . and looked at her some more. *She's pretty*, he thought. But more happened. As they talked, their spirits met. He just knew by her disposition that she was a born-again believer in Christ. Furthermore, she *was* pretty! He also detected that hiding behind her shyness was brilliance. *She is smart . . . very smart*, he noted.

"How old are you?" Ernst asked.

"Twenty-one."

"I'm twenty. I'm a student at Liebenzell, preparing to be a missionary. What are you going to do?"

"Well, I have already qualified for university entrance, since I graduated from high school with honors. But I'm not going away to study yet. My mother's health is weakening, so I'm staying home to help her take care of the house and gardens."

Ernst smiled, thinking, *Beauty, intelligence, dedication to family . . .*

Sigrid continued, "I also lead a children's class in our church and play the organ in the evening fellowship meetings."

"Is that so?" Ernst loosened his collar for air.

"Yes. I'm enjoying serving the Lord in this way for the time being, but I'm waiting to see how He will lead for the future."

As far as Ernst was concerned, only one question still remained: "Did you study Latin?"

"Well, yes, I did. Why do you ask?"

* * *

The celebration dragged on until midnight, but for Ernst the evening was forever young. He and Sigrid exchanged addresses and parted. God smiled, leaving no footprints. Getting Ernst to the wedding had been a task. As he walked into the night, however, Sigrid's eyes kept dancing before him, and he found himself praying, *Lord, is this the woman I am to marry?*

CHAPTER SEVENTEEN

Tough Terms and Tender Love

Ernst had no sooner returned to Bad Liebenzell when summer kicked into high gear. One night he whipped out a pen to write Sigrid a note. Writing about campus activities, he hoped she could detect the deeper message intended by his heart. He mysteriously felt poetry awakening within him—romantic poetry. But he knew it wasn't wise to reveal his feelings just yet.

For three months he kept thinking, *I must see her.* Finally, he connived a reason to visit her home, cloaking his intention as merely a family gesture. Borrowing the seminary's bicycle, he rode eighty miles to Sigrid's home in Villingen.

"Hello, Mr. and Mrs. Schambach. How are you?" he greeted upon arrival.

Stunned at the sudden interest, Walter and Eugenie Schambach responded, "Very well, thank you." Throughout the afternoon and evening, minutes felt like hours while creating "family" talk with the Schambachs. But when Sigrid walked into the room an hour flashed by like a second.

"You cannot ride back tonight," Walter said to Ernst. "It's too far. Sleep here and leave in the morning."

"All right, thank you," he replied without reluctance.

"Your bedroom is at the top of the stairs and to the left," instructed Eugenie. As Ernst ascended the stairs and

Sigrid carried empty cups to the kitchen, Walter and Eugenie looked at Ernst, then at their daughter. Turning to each other, they grinned knowingly.

The next morning, Ernst whistled and pedaled all the way back to Bad Liebenzell. He pumped extra fast and glided down hills with his legs stretched to each side, catching the wind and laughing at the mystically lighthearted, warm feelings he had never known before.

* * *

Graduation came soon. All graduates were required to spend one year as intern pastors to expand their practical education and prove their fitness for service. Ernst took ten fellowship churches under his wing. One of the most thrilling parts was that the distance to the Schambachs' was now reduced to thirty-five miles. Ernst bought a motorcycle to service the fellowships, but it was most often seen heading to Sigrid's home.

"You may visit our daughter anytime," Walter informed Ernest one evening, "but I don't like meetings on the side of the street. You may have the living room all to yourselves. My wife and I will not interfere."

"I will gladly honor and appreciate that, Mr. Schambach."

And so it was that cake and commitment shifted from Willie's table to the Schambachs' living room. In time, the conversation drifted from teasing to serious discussions about the future. Then one evening, Ernst blurted out, "I want to marry you. Will you be my wife?"

There was a frightfully long pause. The answer, "Yes," broke the suspense, "but . . ."

Oh, no, thought Ernst, *a "but." What could be wrong?*

". . . but you must ask my father."

"OK. But I'm afraid. You know my father is so different from your father. What should I say to him?"

"My father will not judge you by your father. Simply tell him why you want me to be your wife, as well as your plans for our future. Then we will see where it goes from there."

The next day Ernst set up a special date on which to speak with Mr. Schambach. He counted the dreaded days and hours leading up to the meeting as one would await execution.

"I will agree for you to marry my daughter." Walter gave his approval, then added, "but not yet. You need time to grow closer, to get to know each other better. It's still too early."

Not sure how to respond, Ernst scratched the back of his head and said, "Thank you, sir. Thank you."

For the following year Ernst pastored the ten fellowship groups and visited the Schambach home. Walter had shown spiritual maturity to receive Ernst as a brother in Christ. It was also wise for him to insist that Ernst and Sigrid take time to develop their relationship. Much discussion would be needed for two people from such divergent backgrounds to adjust.

Ernst was troubled that perhaps he expected Sigrid to give up too much to marry him. He knew she had dated a medical student who could offer her a more affluent life. "Sigrid," he told her one night, "I fear that it's not fair for me to ask you to give up luxury to be my wife."

"Ernst, there's something I have wanted to tell you," Sigrid replied. "Before I ever met you, I felt a clear call from God to be the wife of a missionary. That desire has been in my heart for several years."

Feeling emboldened, Ernst said, "I have been sensing the Lord's leading to be a missionary to Japan." The intoxication of joy made him flippant, as he went on to say, "I will need a healthy wife to go with me." Sigrid fell silent, and the evening ended awkwardly.

Days later a letter from Sigrid arrived at Ernst's apartment, stating that she didn't want to see him anymore. Shocked, Ernst dropped into a chair and took a deep breath. *How could this be? What did I do wrong? Why did she change her mind after all of this time?*

For two weeks he lifelessly slogged through his duties at the fellowship groups. Finally, he phoned Sigrid and said, "Please tell me what is going on. I need to talk to you. May I see you?"

There was a pause. "You may come, but you need to speak to my father before you speak with me."

Ernst lost no time getting to Sigrid's home. Once again Ernst and Walter sat alone in the living room. The ticking of the clock on the wall felt like the sword of Damocles swinging over Ernst's head.

"You told me that you loved my daughter."

"Yes, I do."

"I question that."

Ernst felt his face flush.

"How can you say that you love my daughter, then say that you must have a healthy wife? Why would you make that a stipulation? She is healthy today, but if you do not take Sigrid without any conditions, then you can leave now and never return. You must accept her as she is and leave the future in God's hands. If you don't trust God, then I don't trust you."

Silence reigned. Ernst heard his heart beating. This moment would either transform him or destroy him. His response would determine the difference: Defending himself could mean defeat; humbling himself could mean victory. He didn't sense Walter intending to hurt him, but instead to bring him face-to-face with responsibility.

"Sir, I am sorry. I didn't mean what I said."

"Sorry is all right, but consider your ways. If you really didn't mean it, then you should not have said it. If you did mean it, then it's over. You will not marry my daughter."

Never would Ernst learn a stronger lesson about guarding his words. There was so much at stake. Ernst knew he had found a rare treasure in Sigrid. Her parents had taught her both by instruction and example what God intended a wife to be. She would be a true helpmate, and Ernst was on the verge of losing her. This was the time to speak his heart clearly.

"Sir, I'm sorry. I see the error of my words. Further, I see the importance as never before of saying only what I mean. Please give me another chance."

"Very well, you may speak with my daughter."

Ernst met Sigrid on the porch. Taking her hand in his, he apologized, "Your father told me what I said was wrong. Please believe that I was speaking foolishly, not weighing the importance of my words. I did not mean them. I want you as my wife no matter what happens in the future. If you remain healthy, then that will be wonderful. But if you become ill, then I want the privilege of caring for you. Will you forgive me and marry me?" The answer came as she lay her hand on his. Ernst's humility was genuine and God raised him up again. A thousand choirs burst into song within his heart.

On April 6, 1952, Ernst and Sigrid were officially engaged. But circumstances and thousands of miles would separate them the very next day.

CHAPTER EIGHTEEN

Attacked From the Back

The next morning Ernst departed for England to learn English—not formally, but by speaking the language while living with an English family. That would prove futile, however, since resentment against the Germans remained high after the war, and no English families would accept him. Then a Christian Swiss family living in England, Mr. and Mrs. Hofer, invited Ernst into their home, located between London and Brighton. There was only one problem: They rarely spoke English. So, for the next five months Ernst spoke a lot of German but learned little English.

But he was doggedly committed to fulfilling his mission. He knew that he could expect satanic opposition, since the Bible was clear about the spiritual struggle all believers face. Sitting high on "fire mountain," he had nearly memorized Ephesians 6:10-18 where Paul talks about putting on the whole armor of God to stand against the evil forces that would war against him. He had particularly noted that in verse thirteen Paul did not say "*if* the evil day comes," but rather "*when* the evil day comes." Ernst had already experienced many fiery darts, but never could he have guessed what the first flaming spear would be.

Two short months into his stay, Ernst awoke one June morning barely able to open his eyes or move his head. Splitting pain shot from his back, up his neck and throughout his head. Having never had a headache, he hardly knew what was happening. The thought of getting out of bed seemed impossible. When he did sit up, nausea consumed him.

"Ernst, you must see a doctor," Mrs. Hofer said. "My husband will take you there today."

A lengthy examination ensued that included X rays.

"Ernst," said the doctor, "the news isn't good. The X rays show that your back is disfigured. There are some unusual results with your blood tests too."

"Will I be well soon? I'm leaving for Japan."

"No, no, that's too dangerous," the doctor shook his head. "First, you must have an operation to see if the problem can be corrected."

Stunned, Ernst conceded that he would consider it, and left the doctor's office.

When they returned to the Hofer residence, Ernst phoned Sigrid to tell her the prognosis.

"This is serious, Ernst. I wish I could be there with you. I'll be praying that God will show you what to do. Please know how deeply I love you and miss you."

Later that evening, as Ernst shifted his body seeking some relief from the nagging pain, he remembered a Baptist church he had attended in London. He had gained a deep trust for the pastor there. So, the following Sunday, Ernst approached him at the close of the service.

"Pastor, I am preparing to go to Japan as a missionary. The Liebenzell Mission wanted me to come here first to learn English. Not long ago I began having terrible headaches. The doctor said that it's too dangerous for me to go to Japan and an operation is necessary. Could you have two or three of your church leaders pray for me the way it says in James 5:14-16?"

The hulking pastor smiled broadly, laid his log of an arm around Ernst's shoulders and said, "Gladly. We will do it tonight."

Later, in the pastor's study, he and other church leaders gathered around Ernst and laid hands on him. Although Ernst was not accustomed to people touching him, his hope of being healed far outweighed his cultural inhibition.

"Oh, God," prayed the pastor, "You have brought this brother to salvation and called him to Japan. Now, these terrible headaches threaten to disrupt Your plan. We do not know if these headaches are an attack of the devil or simply physical, but they are about to stop him. Now we are asking You in the name of Jesus Your Son to heal him completely this very night . . . ."

Another prayed, then another. Ernst was struck by the confidence with which they prayed. They approached God with the boldness Ernst had read about in the book of Hebrews.

Finally the last "amen" was said and the pastor turned to Ernst, "Brother, remember to give thanks to the Lord for answering prayer. How He will do it, or when you'll experience it, we don't know. But just give thanks."

Ernst's temples were still thumping, and it seemed strange to be thanking God for something that seemed to have failed. Still he said over and over, "Thank you . . . thank you . . . thank you." This was not a mantra or formula to get God to heal him; it was submission to God, honoring and trusting Him. Ernst thought of the great words of faith spoken by the three Hebrew children before they were thrown into the fiery furnace. They knew God could deliver them, yet they said "but if not" they still would not deny their God. So, not knowing if God would choose to heal him, he repeated, "Thank you . . . thank you. . . ."

The next morning Ernst awoke to a miracle. All the pain was gone! He moved his head from side to side to see if he could find where the pain was hiding. But it wasn't there. It was *gone*! Back to the doctor he went.

Following another battery of tests, including X rays, the doctor sat across from Ernst to deliver the news. "Nothing. I can't see anything that I saw before. Your back has straightened out." Staring at the reports the doctor slowly shook his head. "It's all normal. You can go to Japan."

Ernst stayed in England for two more months. Days before his return to Germany on August 15, he sat in front of Buckingham Palace feeding the birds and thinking back to the time when he nearly lost Sigrid. *Her father was so right to rebuke me. I made the brash statement about needing a healthy wife, and I'm the one who just faced a problem that threatened to stop me from going to Japan. I know Sigrid would stay with me, even if I had not been healed. How foolish I was.*

Then he prayed, *Lord, You have allowed me to experience the power of the enemy hurling a flaming spear. But I refuse to fear him, since I have also experienced Your power to deliver. I will go to Japan trusting You, no matter what may come. But first, I will see Sigrid.*

CHAPTER NINETEEN

The Discipline of Destiny

In August of 1952, Ernst was ready to leave for Japan. "I will write to you every day," he assured Sigrid as they rode the train to Lausanne, Switzerland, where they would again part for the coming year.

"No, you must not. The Bible instructs you to love me. It also teaches me to respect and submit to you. I cannot respect a man who does not fulfill his purpose. I love you and will give myself fully to you and your purpose, but you must prepare to fulfill it. You must study and master the Japanese language. You can't do that while writing letters to me. Write to me once every two weeks."

Ernst looked upon Sigrid with astonishment, realizing again the full measure of his treasure. She was a woman who would help him fulfill God's calling upon his life, a woman who would not let their romance become a god to either of them. Ernst took her hand and quietly watched the hills and valleys pass by the train window. The August heat was cut by a breeze from a slightly opened window. Across from them sat Arthur Kunz, a Swissman who was also going to Japan as a missionary. Arthur's fiancée joined them too.

"Lausanne . . . Lausanne!" bellowed the conductor as the train slowed. Ernst wished that time would stop until he was ready to leave his beautiful Sigrid, but all too soon the doors opened to spill them onto the platform of separation.

Soon Ernst's luggage was transferred to the next train; nothing remained except the dreaded good-bye. Their moment of solace was shattered by a shrill, lonely blast from the train's whistle, signaling the time to board. Ernst took Sigrid into his arms. He wanted to say something noble, but nothing came. He wanted to cry, but dared not. Her eyes were so wide and accepting—full of trust and anticipation. He tried to freeze-frame them into his mind.

The two stood in silence flooded by a sense of oneness. Then Sigrid reached up and brushed her hand through his hair. "You go," she tenderly whispered. "Put your mind and heart into what God wants you to do. I love you and will be praying for you until the day when I can come to you. It will only be one year. That's not so bad."

"I love you, Sigrid."

The train's whistle gave one final call. Ernst took a deep breath, boarded the train and ran to his seat to wave at Sigrid from the window. As the train gained speed, he lost sight of his beloved amid the crowd on the platform. He felt his heart tearing as she slowly slipped from reality into memory.

* * *

"Marseille . . . Marseille . . ." called the conductor. Steam gushed out from under the train and the sound of steel on steel subsided then stalled. Ernst and Arthur disembarked from the train and then lugged their boxes and baggage to the dock. There they would board the *La Marseille*, a ship named after the port city. After a great deal of struggle, their possessions were stacked by a scale and then weighed.

"Your luggage is over the weight limit," said the man weighing the luggage to Ernst, his voice gruff and condemning. "You'll have to pay an additional 600 francs."

Ernst fumbled in his pocket and pulled out the exact amount. He put his hand back into his pocket: empty. He had just the right amount and no more. He smiled.

A deep, forlorn blast from the ship's foghorn pierced the air. The time to board had come. Ernst and Arthur dumped their luggage in their cabin, then ran to the promenade to watch from the deck as the ship left the dock. Gulls swooped through the salty air in search of food thrown by the passengers. Tugboats shoved the ship away from the harbor, and it slowly moved into deep waters. Ernst stood transfixed in thought. All he could see were Sigrid's warm, steady eyes before his mind's eye. Soon he and Sigrid would be separated by the ocean itself.

The two young missionaries returned to their cabin, unsure of what their journey would bring. Days went by. Then one day, as the huge ship lazily glided up the Mekong River toward Saigon, bullets screamed through the air just above their heads. People began to panic and scramble for protection. "Duck! . . . Get down, everybody! Get down!" yelled a shipmate.

"Look," said Arthur, "they're shooting at us from each side of the river. Why?"

"This is a French ship," said a passenger crouching beside them.

"So?" questioned Ernst.

"Vietnam is fighting for independence from France. There are hundreds of French Legionnaires hiding below on this ship. The Vietnamese rebels know it and are showing their resistance."

"Whew!" Ernst said as he wiped his arm across his sweaty brow. He leaned against a steel post, looked up at the sky and thought, *God, You have delivered me from the prison camp, from my health problem and from my sins. You gave me a faithful fiancée. I have made a commitment to You, and I know You will be faithful in Your commitment to me. Therefore, I rest assured that You will get me safely to Japan for Your purposes.*

The shooting died away, and the Legionnaires disembarked at Saigon. Soon Ernst and Arthur were sailing for Japan. Ernst used part of his time to mark his calendar, circling the dates when he would write to Sigrid.

Within days they saw the ocean crashing onto the shores of Japan, and Ernst's preconceived ideas surrendered to reality. The first two years would be devoted to learning the language. That would be hard, but nothing in comparison to the deeper lessons to be learned through the clash of cultures. He had assumed that he was going to Japan as a Christian missionary, when in fact he was a *German* Christian missionary in Japan. Only God could sort out the differences between the two.

CHAPTER TWENTY

The German in Japan

"Hello, I'm Ernst Vatter." Smiling broadly Ernst thrust his hand toward Rev. Otto Mosimann, expecting a hearty handshake. Otto, who was a Swiss serving as the Liebenzell Mission field director in Japan, stood motionless. Ernst cleared his throat, then awkwardly withdrew his hand, wondering what he had done wrong.

The director then bent slightly at the waist and gently bobbed his head a few times. "Welcome, Ernst," he said, placing his hand on Ernst's shoulder as they walked away from the ship. "Now is the time for you to learn a most important thing about being a missionary. Christ left heaven in order to become like us. Only then could He make us like Himself. Likewise, to be a missionary in Japan you must enter this culture, leaving yours behind. Germans shake hands when they greet; Japanese do not. They show honor by bowing to each other."

"So, the days of a good handshake are over?" queried Ernst in a mischievous tone. He had learned his first lesson.

Soon Ernst was unpacking his few clothes and lining his many books on the shelves of his room at the mission compound. Located in Nakanoshima, a small village at the northern edge of the big city of Kawasaki, the compound sat close to the banks of the Tama River, marking the border between Tokyo and the Kanagawa Province.

Two days after arriving, Ernst sat at breakfast receiving directions from Otto about the various trains to take to go to the Naganuma Language School. "They're expecting you," he said. Ernst's eyes glazed as he mouthed the directions back to Otto, replete with names he could hardly pronounce. Shortly after, he boarded the train and watched a new world scroll past his window. He was about to learn the language that would enable him to communicate in a world of new smells, sounds, sights, dress and mannerisms. *Pay attention and learn well,* he told himself. *You don't want to end up like that other missionary . . .*

The story had become infamous. A young man at the mission was studying Japanese. Eager to share his faith and show off his newfound language skills, he stood on a busy street corner distributing tracts. "Please read this," he boldly declared in Japanese to each passerby. But his attempt to Christianize the culture was eliciting an odd response. The men, and many of the women, would look down at the ground, not even acknowledging him. All of the young girls would giggle and hide their faces as they quickly shuffled past. It was not until much later in the day that a very red-faced, but wiser, man realized he had instead been saying, "Please become my fiancée." The tale stood as a lesson and a warning to all new arrivals to the mission—one that Ernst planned to heed in the weeks and months ahead.

"This culture seems so fragile, Rev. Mosimann," Ernst observed. "My German heritage feels more rugged. Germans walk with determination while the Japanese gingerly shuffle along. We speak firmly where they speak softly. We laugh openly where they muffle it."

"Yes, it's true. This is all foreign to the way you think. It's tempting to view your background as superior, but it's not; it is only different. As you learn the motivations behind Japanese ways you'll find some of them are better than your own. Above all, you must resolve in your heart to let go of your German past and wholeheartedly enter into the Japanese way of life. Otherwise there will be no way to share the gospel with them."

Ernst was experiencing his third birth. The first was his natural birth into a German family. The second was his spiritual birth into God's kingdom. Now, he was being laboriously born into the Japanese culture.

Three months of schooling had passed when once again Ernst opened his calendar, delighted to see it was one of the days to write to Sigrid. The bustling world outside of his apartment became silent as he got alone with his thoughts. With pen in hand, he shaped his future with words.

My dearest Sigrid, There is no way to express how deeply I long to see you. The months drag by like years. I so look forward to your joining me in Japan just nine months from now.

You were right to encourage me to write only once every two weeks. Not only do I put more time into learning the language, but it helps me not to write about my first impressions, for they are often wrong. I have learned the lesson that cultures are distinct, but not superior. I realize that I cannot effectively present the gospel until I fully respect and honor this culture that is foreign to mine. I don't want you to come here with your mind cluttered by my misjudgments.

Slowly I'm letting go of my German way of thinking and adopting theirs. It's like breathing underwater with a scuba tank. It seems strange, even scary at first, but eventually it becomes natural. One thing I will never get over, however, is my love for you.

Ernst folded the letter and placed it in an envelope. He pictured Sigrid's face and counted the months until they would be together again. . . .

* * *

One morning, two months later, Otto was awakened early by deep moans coming from Ernst's room. Upon entering, he found Ernst in bed, his skin sweaty and ashen.

"What's wrong, Ernst?"

"I don't know. I have terrible pain near my stomach," Ernst said, clutching at his abdomen.

"It could be appendicitis. We must rush you to the hospital. Move as little as possible. I'll help you to the car."

Flinging Ernst's arm over his shoulder, Otto dragged him to the car and hurried through the narrow streets to the Seibo Hospital. For one hour Ernst writhed in pain as Otto drove and the infection worsened. By the time they arrived at the hospital, Ernst's clothes were soaked with perspiration.

Tests were run as swiftly as possible and soon the doctor was barking orders to his staff. "Inflamed appendix. Emergency surgery," the doctor said. The nurse immediately wheeled Ernst to a dimly-lit room with a large bright light looming over an uncomfortably hard bed.

Following the operation, Ernst was groggily watching the world slowly refocus, when one of his instructors from the language school came to his bedside. He was comforted by

Nestled in the Alb Mountains of southwestern Germany is the small town of Goenningen, Germany, where Ernst spent his childhood.

The Vatter family (front row L to R) Mother (Ernstine), Hedwig (oldest child and only daughter), Father (Victor); (back row L to R) Berthold, the fifth child (passed away on his 50th birthday), Otto (oldest son and second child, deceased), Horst (third child, for whom Ernst was falsely identified and arrested; he is still missing in the former USSR), Ernst (fourth child), and Kraft (youngest and sixth child).

Ernst returns to the home of his parents. The lower right door was the stable entrance for horses his father raised. As a child, Ernst was terrified of horses.

Aunt Sofie, Ernst and Uncle Ernst pose for a formal portrait. This is the aunt and uncle with whom Ernst chose to live at the age of two. Aunt Sofie was the sister of Ernst's father, Victor.

Ernst (pointing to his upstairs bedroom) has many pleasant memories of those childhood years. He was living here when he was wrongfully arrested by the French soldiers at the end of World War II.

The night of his arrest, Ernst was imprisoned in this former German soldier barracks in Tuebingen. This is where he first witnessed the degrading treatment people impose upon one another.

Released by the French officers, he returned home by foot. Despite the risk, Ernst and two other soldiers stopped at this Lutheran manse in Kuppingen, the home of Rev. Erhard and Elizabeth Eisenman. Mrs. Eisenman salved and bound Ernst's bruised and bleeding feet.

Willie and Clara Klein were committed to Christ and to each other. Willie became Ernst's spiritual counselor, and was used by God to direct Ernst in his early Christian years. Recently, Ernst visited Clara who had served young Ernst cake and milk while her husband discipled the eager new believer.

From atop the Bad Liebenzell Castle, we look down on the campus of the Liebenzell Mission. Many of the buildings were erected under Ernst's direction. It is from here that he and Sigrid were commissioned to Japan for twelve years of missionary service, and where for twenty-four years he served as the Overseas Director of the Mission.

One of the main buildings, which for years housed both seminary classrooms and offices, looks like an elaborate alpine ski lodge. Ernst's office on the top floor could be reached only by a long and steep staircase.

Aunt Sofie and Sigrid, then Ernst's fiancée, bid farewell to him in 1952 as he left for his first missionary assignment in Japan.

Since there were no paved roads outside of town, Ernst's evangelistic trips to the Japanese countryside required that he travel by motorcycle.

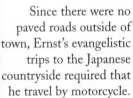

In Japan, on December 16, 1954, Ernst and Sigrid exchanged marriage vows. The field director, Rev. Ettling, seen here with his wife, performed the wedding in a Japanese church.

During the Vatters' first six-year term, the Lord blessed them with Norman (left, born 1956) and Iris (far right, born 1957). Anette was born (1961) after the family returned for their second six-year term.

Evelyne (born 1964) completed the Vatter family.

The Vatter family in later years (L to R): Ernst, Iris (in nurses' training), Evelyne (in high school), Norman (a university student), Sigrid (called "Mum") and Anette (in high school).

Ernst interviews missionaries during a mission convention that nearly 5,000 people attended.

Ernst and Sigrid celebrate their silver wedding anniversary.

Ernst ministers on the Island of Manus in the Pacific Islands. Rev. Hubert Charles, pastor of the Palau Evangelical Church, greets him, along with the youth pastor.

The Vatters' oldest daughter, Iris, is a missionary to Burundi. She served as the translator for Bishop Pie of the Burundi Anglican Church during his visit to the Liebenzell Mission headquarters.

The Vatters' younger daughter, Evelyne, and husband, Markus, serve as missionaries in Botswana where Markus is a missionary pilot. Their children (L to R): Elisabeth, Johannes and Daniel.

Norman and his family live in Munich where Norman is the chief officer of security for the huge pipeline at Ingolstadt, Bavaria. L to R: Jachin, Aileen, Cathrin, Mirijam, Anika, Norman, Conny, Samuel and Michael.

This is the hospital where Ernst escaped death at the age of 29. Here on the balcony of this same hospital, he reflects upon his struggle for life that to this day, forty years later, causes relapses and imposes physical limitations on him.

Rev. Harada is the current Executive Director of the Liebenzell Mission in Japan. He is responsible for all Japanese missionaries who serve with the Mission.

At the airport in Ulan Bator, Mongolia, Rev. Detlef Krause, Ernst's successor, greets a Japanese missionary working in that country.

Ernst visits the island of West New Britian, Papua New Guinea where he is greeted with fresh floral leis.

Liebenzell Mission International delegates from the U.S., Canada, Switzerland, Austria and Japan gather in Taiwan for a triennial conference. Ernst pictured in the center.

Ernst (back center) served for six years as the chairman of the Missions Commission of World Evangelical Fellowship at Liebenzell.

Detlef Krause, seen here with his wife, Esther, took Ernst's place as Overseas Director of the Mission. He continues to serve in that position at the time of this writing.

An intense expression crossed Ernst's face as Sigrid told her side of their story. She spoke of the blessings, frustrations and disappointments she faced serving as the wife of this aggressive leader. Ernst was surprised to learn that she once wept secretly as he departed for yet another trip. "Being interviewed for this book is good," he said. "I'm hearing things I never knew before." Something sacred unfolded as the Vatters learned about each other on new and deeper levels.

Ernst and Sigrid stand in the doorway of their home in Calw. Outside this home, Ernst led a global mission. Behind the door, however, he felt as though he always had something new to learn from his wife and best friend.

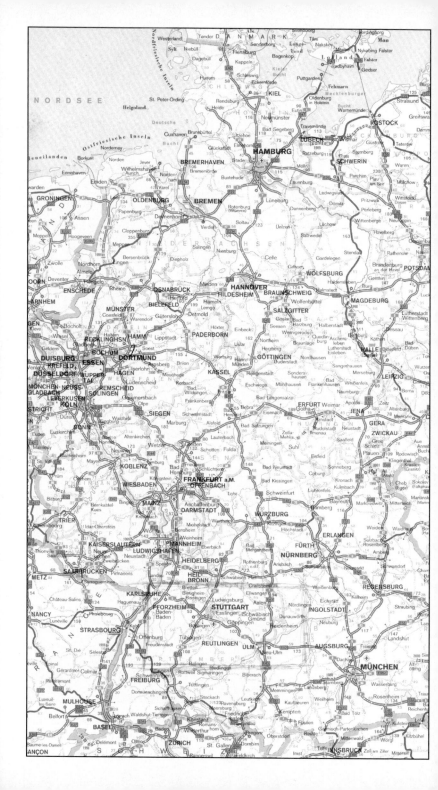

the sight of a familiar face. They spoke briefly, then she departed. A few days later she returned. As they talked, she began to laugh. "When I visited you the first time, Mr. Vatter, we had a short conversation, but you were still under the effects of the anesthesia."

"Did I say anything stupid?"

"No, no, no," she laughed, "but you did sound funny. Actually, I was impressed that you spoke to me in very good Japanese. What you have been learning has found its way deep into your subconscious mind. You spoke very well. Now I know that you will master the Japanese language."

Ernst was feeling better about his growing ability to lay aside the garment of his German culture and don the robes of Japanese culture. A couple of months later, however, he experienced another physical setback. This time, he had difficulty swallowing. He was taken to the hospital, where it was discovered he had tonsilitis and would require surgery again. The operation would not be done on a hard bed but in a chair that was laid back almost flat.

"Open wide," said Doctor Eitel, another German in Japan. A needle was inserted to inject a painkiller on both sides of his throat. All went well on the first side, but not so with the other. Dr. Eitel inserted the needle, paused, then exclaimed, "It's stuck and the syringe came off the needle!"

"Can you reconnect them?" a nurse asked.

"No, get me those pliers."

Ernst's eyes shot wide open.

"Don't move." said Doctor Eitel. "Don't shut your mouth. Just be quiet. There . . . I got the needle out. Now we can operate, but I cannot numb the other side."

Ernst's eyes opened wider still, and the reddened tonsil thumped even harder. The painkiller sat useless on a shelf while the doctor removed the tonsils—one with painkiller and the other without. For several days after surgery, just the simple act of drinking water felt like swallowing broken glass. His suffering through both the appendicitis and tonsilitis, however, did what strength could not do; it endeared him to the Japanese people and them to him.

Near the end of his first year in Japan, as Ernst's anticipation of seeing Sigrid grew, he and Arthur Kunz decided to distribute Christian tracts in a farming area about an hour's drive from the mission. They crossed fields going from village to village. Ernst, always in a hurry, took a shortcut through the back yard of one farmer's home. That's when it happened. He took several steps, feeling the mushy ground sag beneath him. Suddenly there was a snap, and Ernst dropped through some rotten planks.

"Arthur! Arthur! Come, help me!"

Arthur raced toward Ernst's panic-stricken voice. As he rounded the corner of the house, he saw Ernst standing thigh deep in a cesspool. The family and neighbors knew that the boards were rotten, and they avoided the cesspool. But Ernst innocently stepped on it and found himself at a new and unintended level of entering a different culture.

"Oh! . . . oh! . . . oh!" exclaimed the woman of the house as she shuffled toward him. Arthur, laughing so as to nearly lose his strength, mustered enough to pull Ernst out.

"I'm so sorry," continued the woman. "Please come into my house. I will give you my husband's kimono to wear after you wash. I will wash your clothes and shoes."

Hours later, Ernst and Arthur drove back to the mission compound. Ernst was somber and quiet while Arthur's cheeks were ready to explode with laughter.

"Arthur, I've never been so humiliated in all my life."

"Well, that's about as close to anyone's culture as you'll ever come," laughed Arthur.

"I don't think this is part of entering a culture. One thing is sure, that dear lady certainly cared for me despite the fact that I ruined their cesspool. We are here to show her the love of God, but the tables were turned and she certainly showed love to me." The setting sun felt good on his shoulders, comforting his embarrassed soul.

By year's end, Ernst had adopted a new culture, developed a taste for new food, spoke a new language, lost his appendix and tonsils and learned to watch where he stepped. His advancements far outweighed his struggles. With his whole world changing, he clung to the constants in his life—his commitment to God and his love for Sigrid.

Sigrid! There was a redeeming thought. Twelve months and twenty-six letters later he was rushing to the dock to greet her.

CHAPTER TWENTY-ONE

The Bench of Dreams

"There she is!" Ernst blurted as Sigrid exited the ship. The people around him smiled, recognizing the enthusiasm of a young man in love. The couple embraced at the bottom of the gangplank.

Suddenly, the difficulty of the year's separation evaporated like mist in the sun. Ernst looked into Sigrid's round face and fawn-colored eyes, knowing that behind her shy facade was a tenacious spirit, a strong woman, the kind needed to assist him in his commitment to the gospel. After a kiss and another long hug, they walked hand in hand into their future.

"Where will I stay?" asked Sigrid.

"You will take my place at the mission compound. I've already moved in with Pastor Tanaka in Eifuku-cho, a section of Tokyo. It's about a forty-five minute train ride from the mission compound. At the end of each week I'll come to see you."

"That will be wonderful," Sigrid said in her sweet, soft voice. By day's end, she was settled into the compound and Ernst had returned to his apartment. That night he was lying in his bed thinking, and found himself praying aloud . . .

123

"My kind Heavenly Father, You have been so good to me. You began leading me to Yourself when I was only two. You knew that Aunt Sofie would do all in her power to bring me to the gospel. Then You led me through the prison camp, only to humble me and prepare me to respond to You. I shall never forget the fresh wind that blew through my heart the night I said yes to You.

"Then You would not give me peace about serving within the state structure of the Lutheran Church; rather, You pressed me to walk a less trodden path—one that has forced me to trust You more completely. Now You have brought Sigrid in preparation to serve with me. She is still as beautiful in person as she was in my memory. Thank You . . . thank You. Help us honor and glorify You in this year of courtship, then in our marriage." Slowly his voice drifted into silence. He slept deeply.

Several days later, Ernst and Sigrid boarded the train for Tokyo where they planned to take a stroll through the city. Looking out the train window, Ernst spotted a bench by the Todai Station. Tall university buildings stood behind it, and smaller buildings crouched around it. Sunlight streamed down between the buildings, bathing the bench like a solitary garden of romance.

"Let's get off here," he blurted, grabbing Sigrid's hand and dashing for the door. Once on the platform, Sigrid looked questioningly at Ernst.

"Look, Sigrid. See this bench? It looks so warm and inviting. Let's make this *our* bench. We can meet here each time you come to Tokyo. Now, let's sit down and talk. How are you doing with your language study?"

"I'm really enjoying my private tutoring at the mission," Sigrid replied, then asked, "Do you find it beneficial to have only six people in your class at the language school?"

"Yes," Ernst replied. "The classes have always been small so that each student gets personal attention. What do you think about their changing my instructors each hour?"

"Amazing. That way you won't develop a particular accent."

"It's true. By the way, I have some silly stories to tell you about my past year here in Japan." Sigrid laughed heartily as Ernst told her about falling into the farmer's cesspool.

They talked for hours until a shadow slowly slid up the side of the building behind them, signaling it was time to go. Just before they boarded the train, Ernst said, with a twinkle in his eye, "I'm glad you didn't say we can only sit on this bench and talk once every two weeks."

"Oh, Ernst, it was for the best," Sigrid replied with a smile. "But now it's different—we're together. We must go now and do our homework. They certainly pile on a lot of work, but that's good."

In the days and weeks to come, their bench became the scene of many talks about God, about life and about their future.

As Ernst and Sigrid's first year of courtship drew to a close, and the day of their marriage neared, Ernst was pulled into a situation that heightened his discernment between the unexplainable and the demonic. He was summoned to the home of Rev. Ettling, the acting field director of the Liebenzell Mission.

"Ernst, we are having a serious problem. A missionary serving at our station at Yuki believes there is a demon in his home. He hears things at night. He is frightened for his family's sake and is ready to leave the field if we don't help him. Tonight we will go to his home to pray."

That night they were greeted by the missionary. He looked ashen and tired. His wife stood by his side, her eyes mixed with fear, fatigue and hope—hope that Ernst and Rev. Ettling could bring deliverance.

"It's our children," she said. "We don't want anything to harm our children. We have prayed and prayed, but the demon still persists. It's terrifying, especially when prayer doesn't seem to help. Not only do we hear sounds of movement, but soft voices also come from strange directions, and the sound of footsteps too."

"It may be a long night," said the husband. "The demon generally comes around midnight."

For several hours they talked about the missionary's ministry. They almost forgot the purpose of their visit as the hour hand neared 12 o'clock. Suddenly they heard a *thump!* Something heavy dropped on the roof just above their heads. The missionary's wife grabbed her husband's hand, the hair on her arms bristling. The thump, however, was followed by silence—eerie silence. Then there was a sliding sound, which would abruptly start and stop. It was unsettling for all in the room to think that a power of darkness was so close, embodied and making noise. Rev. Ettling prayed aloud.

"Father, we are here under Your mercy and care. We accept by faith Your provisions for protection, such as the armor of Christ; and, according to Isaiah, give You glory as our rear guard. We also accept by faith that You have given us Your Son's authority to deal with the unseen enemies of the cross. In light of all Your promises and provisions that have been signed and sealed in the blood of Your Son, we ask You to point Your finger and rebuke this power of darkness, forbidding him to return to this home ever again."

The two men fervently prayed until 1 o'clock. Finally, all fell silent. The power seemed to depart. However, less than one week later Rev. Ettling and Ernst were summoned to the home again. The "demon" had returned. That night, both the missionary and his wife were issuing an ultimatum: "Either the demon leaves or we leave!" The muscles in their necks were taut and their voices pinched. Exhausted from frustration and fear, they stood rigid in their resolve. Again a long evening of prayer ended in silence and a seeming end to the problem.

But two weeks later it recurred. Once again Ernst and Rev. Ettling went to the home to pray. As the evening drew to a close, the missionary looked the pastor in the eye and issued his final, nonnegotiable declaration: "Tomorrow we pack!" Within days, the frightened family was gone.

Soon after, Ernst and Rev. Ettling met for lunch. Rev. Ettling was a highly disciplined man, though most friendly and encouraging. His former orientation to China often led to difficulties in his leadership in Japan. Still, Ernst honored him as his superior.

"Ernst," Ettling began, "I think you should move from Makabe to Yuki. I want you to take the mission station that was just vacated. You're soon to marry, and this will give you a place to begin your ministry."

"Move into the demon house?"

"Yes."

"Why not? I'm not convinced it's a demon anyway. Surely if it were a demon, it would have to bow to God and surrender the house." Ernst laughed, "Just wait until I tell Sigrid about our live-in ghost."

The next day, Ernst met Sigrid at their bench. "Sigrid, I have some interesting news for you. I have been asked to take the mission station that was just deserted. I'll be moving there immediately."

"Then I'm going to give you a gift to keep you company until I come to be with you."

"What's that?"

"A kitten."

"A kitten?" Ernst questioned, trying not to reveal his minimal interest in cats. *Why couldn't she have said a puppy?* he thought. *I know she loves cats, but I don't. I must not disappoint her, however.* Love was teaching him an invaluable lesson: One must often set personal preferences aside for the sake of another.

"That's great, Sigrid," he heard himself saying. "That way the kitten will be waiting for you when we marry."

"Yes, and what about the other uninvited guest?" she questioned with a humor that rivaled Ernst's.

"He'll never stand up to a cat," Ernst replied. They laughed.

Sigrid wasn't laughing inside however. She was aware of the seriousness of demons. When she returned to the mission she rushed into her room, fell on her knees and prayed, "Lord, if I am to go to Yuki, then You must drive out the demon before I enter the house. I am trusting You to do this and want to thank You in advance. Amen."

Two weeks later Ernst moved into the mission home. The first thing he did was set the ground rules with the kitten. Looking into its large innocent eyes, he directed, "You and I will get along just fine. But you are here for Sigrid, not me. You will not eat on the table, but only in that corner. You are not to sleep in bed with me. I'll give you a nice soft spot of your own."

Two huge green eyes stared at him with seeming understanding as he finished his speech. "I am in charge of saving souls. You are in charge of catching mice. And both of us are in charge of catching the demon. OK, that's it for now. Let's go to bed."

Ernst and the kitten settled into their separate beds. Then ... *thump*! Ernst was awakened suddenly in the middle of the night. He sat up.

Not seeing anything, he climbed out of bed and walked around the room wondering what the strange intrusion could be. This night, the encounter included soft, indistinguishable voices and footsteps.

"All right, Lord, I need a revelation. Show me what this is." Going outside, he climbed a lattice to the roof. Just as he peered over the edge, he saw a long, furry creature rushing off the other side.

"Marten! You're a marten, not a demon! You've been jumping on my ceiling to catch little rodents. And just think, while catching rodents you drove off a missionary! Tomorrow I'll put something on the roof to drive you away."

Next, Ernst had to solve the mystery of the voices and footsteps. Finally, some nights later the revelation came to him. "Ahhh, now I know what those voices and footsteps are," he said to the cat purring on his lap. "It's the wind carrying the noises of the large family next door through the hallway. The doors and windows are made of very thin glass, so the sounds seem to be right here in our house. When the wind stops we can't hear them. When the wind blows, we do. Mystery solved!"

He put his feline roommate to bed, crawled into his own bed and slept in triumph. The ordeal was over. Indeed, Ernst knew that demons were real, and that someday he might have to deal with them, but he learned to demystify the unexplainable before concluding that a problem was demonic.

The next time he met Sigrid she asked, "Well, Ernst, will I have to come and live with a demon?"

"Just one," Ernst laughed, "but I'll change." Sitting on the bench hand-in-hand, they continued talking about their future.

CHAPTER TWENTY-TWO

German Bells in Japan

December 16, 1954, was a cool day bathed with sunlight. For Ernst and Sigrid it would be a day gilded by love's fulfillment—the two would become one. They rode together in a car to Rev. Matsui's church in Tokyo, while missionary associates boarded a bus at the mission station to attend the ceremony performed by Rev. Ettling.

The couple had taken vows at the Noborito City Hall two days earlier to satisfy Japanese law, but today was their sacred wedding. Ernst and his bride stood around the corner of the church awaiting a regal call—German wedding bells. Sigrid's father had sent a tape of the bells from her home church. Though their parents could not attend the wedding, the bells underscored the blessing Sigrid's parents had placed upon the marriage.

Following the ceremony, everyone returned to the mission headquarters where they feasted on Vienna sausage and potato salad bought at a German butcher shop. The event was topped off with cake and coffee, then the newly married couple departed for a five-day honeymoon in Atami, a hot spring resort on a shore south of Tokyo. On this day the once grumpy groomsman was transformed into a broadly smiling groom. The words "I do" released him from his bachelor co-coon to sprout the wings of a proud young husband.

Six days later, Ernst and Sigrid arrived at their home in Yuki. Fellow missionary Arthur Kunz was there to greet them. He helped carry their luggage into the house, then departed. Finally, they were alone. The peal of the wedding bells was still resonating despite the crude realities of the life that awaited them. . . .

"Ernst, everything is so dusty."

"Oh yes, I forgot to tell you about that. It's from the road outside. We'll be dusting all the time."

Sigrid picked up the kitty that was nearing cathood. "Is it always so dark in here? It's the middle of the day and it's dark."

"Yes, it's always dark in here. It's because of the closeness of the buildings around us. It's always noisy, too, as the windows and doors are so thin. You can hear people sneeze in the day and snore at night."

Sigrid, who had forfeited the lifestyle of the rich, took a deep breath and said, "So be it. Let's start making it home." A flurry of activity erupted. Flowers appeared on the table. The bed was properly made for the first time.

"Grab that broom, Ernst, and sweep. I'll dust."

Ernst knew this was not the time to discuss duties, just obey—which he did. Dustcloths were shaken out the window, dishes were washed and arranged in the cupboard. Ernst brightened to see the changes wrought in their small home, thinking to himself, *So this is how things should have looked all along!* Clothes were unpacked, washed, ironed and placed in drawers. At long last the tired newlyweds sat down to a late dinner.

"Whew, I think I better stay with the work of the churches," Ernst laughed. "It's not nearly as tiring."

Sigrid winked. "After watching you do housework, I can think of a few other reasons why you better stay with the church work!"

* * *

Ernst and Sigrid's faith was to be severely tested as they set out to rebuild the Yuki church. It had been emptied by the paranoia created by the missionary who insisted his house had a demon. For one month only two people attended the weekly meetings: Ernst and Sigrid. Often they prayed in tears. Sometimes they questioned whether or not to stay. Then, one day it happened: A fifteen-year-old girl knocked on the door.

"Pastor Vatter, I want to attend your church."

"Oh, my dear, you are like a ray of sunshine coming through dark storm clouds. You are most welcome."

Then a couple of weeks later an eighteen-year-old girl attended—and became a believer. The following week, she entered, sobbing. "My father is the head of the Buddhist temple," she told Ernst and Sigrid. "He was enraged when he learned of my new faith. He told me that he is ashamed of me, that I'm a disgrace to my family."

At age nineteen that young Christian girl contracted polio, which paralyzed her on one side. When Ernst learned that her father was going to throw her out of the house, he confronted him in holy boldness.

"I'm taking your daughter to the police hospital today," he said as he wrapped the girl in a blanket and lifted her from a cushion on the floor. "I've cleared it with the head physician."

"Our gods are after her!" shouted her father. "It's all your fault that she became a Christian. You must get out of this house before the gods become angry enough to make all of us ill!"

With that, Ernst was gone. For weeks the father's fury thundered throughout the neighborhood, railing against Ernst.

In time the weather grew cold and Christmas was at hand. It was sharply frigid the night a knock came to the parsonage door. Ernst opened it and was shocked to see the girl's mother. She had attended some Christian services but gave no sign of interest.

"Rev. Vatter," she said, taking a half step backward. "I know it's late, but may I come in?"

"Yes, yes, of course."

After much hesitancy the woman blurted, "How can I get the Jesus my daughter has?"

Ernst and Sigrid's eyes met in disbelief. The woman continued.

"You see, every other day I have been traveling 100 kilometers by railroad to see my daughter. Sometimes I sit on her bed and cry. I know that nobody will marry a girl flawed by polio, and an unmarried daughter is a disgrace to a well-respected family. My daughter pats my hand and says, 'Mama, my Lord Jesus will put everything right. He will care for me. Don't be afraid.' I've been strong all my life, but I've never seen strength like this which keeps my daughter strong. Please tell me how I can get this Jesus in my life."

Sigrid took the lady's tiny hands and said, "Pray this after me: 'Dear Heavenly Father, I know that I am a sinner needing Your forgiveness. I am trusting this night that Your Son

Jesus died to take my sins away. Tonight I devote myself to Him to love and serve Him the rest of my life. Amen.' "

The woman repeated the words after Sigrid, then she looked up, her eyes rimmed with tears. "Mrs. Vatter, may I show you something alone?" Ernst quietly left the room, and the woman let her dress slip down her back.

Sigrid choked back tears of her own as she traced the black and blue welts where the woman had been beaten by her husband. "Oh, dear," she said. "I'm so sorry."

"He has done this because I've been attending church services in search of this Jesus. Now I love my Lord and will be faithful to Him even if my husband kills me."

Eventually, the girl recovered from polio, except for a weakness in her right arm. One day she gave a testimony in the little church. "As you know, I had polio. God used that to bring my mother to salvation in Christ. Although my right arm can lift nothing, my mother has been lifted to the right hand of God in Christ. My suffering was worth it all."

This became one of Ernst and Sigrid's most treasured experiences in Japan. Such grand victories, however, didn't remove the struggle of spiritual growth for Ernst. Becoming a saint happens in an instant, the very instant God declares one to be a saint through the sacrificial obedience of Jesus Christ. Learning to live in that sainthood, however, is a lifetime battle. Ernst was committed to serve God with all of his heart, but he continued to find the process of passing from being a *German* Christian to just being a Christian most difficult.

CHAPTER TWENTY-THREE

A Straightforward Blunder

"Seeing people accept Christ has filled me with new energy," Ernst told Sigrid. He threw himself furiously into pastoring the Yuki church while starting two others: one in Iwai and the other in Tochigi. The first was forty miles away and the latter fifty.

People became converts in different ways. For instance, one day a man came to the Vatter home to install new windows in an effort to reduce the dust. Ernst talked to the man about salvation through Jesus alone. Several weeks later there was an urgent knocking on the door. It was the window man.

"Well, what a surprise to see you here today. What can I do for you?" Ernst asked.

"Mr. Vatter, you told me that God sees everything."

"Yes, that's true."

"Today, I went to a brothel. That's doubly horrible since I'm a married man. As soon as I entered, I thought about your words. I realized that God was seeing me. I departed immediately to come and see you. Tell me about God."

Soon, Ernst and the man were on their knees. The man confessed his sins and looked to Christ's death on the cross to take away his sins. He became a regular attendee of the church in Yuki.

On another occasion, while Ernst was passing out tracts in Iwai, a woman approached him and said, "There is a Christian around here whom we call 'Mr. America.' He's Japanese—a farmer—but that's what we call him. I think you should visit him."

Ernst went to Mr. America's little farm. He was thin, bent from hard work and age, but bright. Both his eyes and his personality sparkled with warmth. He made Ernst feel trusted—welcomed.

"Hello, I'm Ernst Vatter with the Liebenzell Mission. I am trying to start a church in this area. Could you help me?"

The man's leathery hands shot toward the sky as he exclaimed, "Praise God! I'm so glad He sent you to me. I am also a Christian and have been asking God to establish a church here in my area. This is indeed an answer to prayer. My heart is overwhelmed with praise to God for this meeting."

Some weeks later as Ernst and Mr. America were talking and praying, the Japanese gentleman said, "Ernst, I want to give that piece of land over there for the new church. I know where there is a storage shed nearby that we can move to serve as the building."

And so it was that a church was planted in Iwai. Within a year thirty converts were on fire with the gospel of Jesus Christ. Mr. America's faithful prayers had been answered.

One night, as Ernst was riding his bicycle home, he punctured a tire on a sharp stone. It was too late to get it repaired. Then he heard a man's voice calling out from a nearby home. "You must come and stay with us tonight. You can get your tire repaired in the morning. There is no way to have it done now."

Soon Ernst was enjoying the warmth of the entire family—strangers turned friends. They talked for a while, then the husband said, "There's the bath. You can clean up before we eat."

Ernst looked across the room. There indeed was the bath, but it was in full view of everyone. Deciding it would be a violation of their culture to refuse, Ernst maneuvered as discreetly as possible, bathing while the family went on talking just across the room. Although they talked to him as he bathed, they kept their eyes averted, acting as though he was not there. Soon he finished, ate and went to bed. He lay thinking how Sigrid would have a long laugh when told about the bath.

At the church in Yuki, a young Japanese graduate from the Bible school was sent to work with Ernst. Ernst noticed that he spent all of his time reading and thinking, and did not follow Ernst's instructions to visit homes and distribute tracts.

"Why aren't you working as I have instructed you?" Ernst demanded one day.

"Well, sir, Jesus didn't begin his ministry until he was thirty years of age. Therefore, I don't think I should either. I am using all of my time to prepare."

Fire raged in Ernst's eyes. Pointing a finger of condemnation at the young man, Ernst replied, "That's nonsense! You were given instructions, and I expect you to follow them. This is little more than an excuse for laziness."

The meeting ended with the air frozen. The young man meekly departed. Ernst felt justified, but in time Pastor Goto came to discuss the incident.

"Ernst, I understand your frustration, but you deeply hurt that young man by the way you spoke. That was not right. You may have destroyed him for ministry. Your straightforward German ways may be upright, but they must be tempered or you will harm the very people you are trying to help. You're too demanding. You must guide him slowly, gently, the same as Jesus does with you."

A wave of memory took Ernst back to the time when he had served the ten fellowships with Rev. Karl Kissling. He could almost feel the pain and humiliation that shot through him the day that the pastor thundered, "You're too proud! Too self-willed! Too immature!" Pastor Kissling could have broken him, just as Ernst could break this young man. Immediately, he determined not to reincarnate Kissling but rather reproduce Christlikeness.

"You're right. I was angry and spoke harshly. That was unwise. I will apologize to him . . . try to make it right and learn from this."

"Thank you, Ernst. That is the sign of spiritual maturity. I, too, will encourage him."

That was Ernst's first encounter with the repercussions of his anger, but it was not yet enough to remove his blunt way of dealing with people. It happened again when he became frustrated with a Sunday school teacher who did not do her job as Ernst thought it should have been done.

"I don't want you to do it that way, Katano. Do it as I have taught you," Ernst scolded.

Ernst was surprised when he no longer saw the woman. Within days Rev. Goto was meeting with him again.

"Ernst, you spoke to Katano as a subordinate. You disgraced her with your sharp rebuke. One of the worst things you can do in Japanese culture is to cause one to lose face."

"I will go and make it right," said the forthright German.

"No, no, you mustn't. That will make it worse. To confront her now is not good. You must speak through another person."

"Oh, my. This is so different from my culture. You would be amazed if you knew how boldly my father-in-law spoke to me over something I said to his daughter. We Germans are a blunt lot. I'm slowly learning the difference between uprightness and straightforwardness, but it's a slow and difficult process. Please help me with Katano."

It wasn't easy for Ernst to admit his error, but he remembered Otto's words when he had arrived—that German culture is different, not superior. And, if he wanted to reach these people, he'd have to lay aside his culture for theirs.

Following lengthy discussions mediated by Rev. Goto, Katano returned to her work at the church. In time, Ernst realized that her way was better than his way since she knew her culture.

One evening, as the sun slowly sank into the west, Ernst sat thinking about the whole experience. *It is so difficult*, he pondered, *to work through an intercessor to right a wrong in this culture. But that's the way it is with God. No one can run into the presence of our holy God without being assisted by our high priest and intercessor Jesus Christ. Perhaps this culture is closer to the divine way than mine.* He found himself understanding the protocol of heaven a little better.

On March 17, 1956, the sounds of the neighbor's children were increased by the cries of the Vatters' own firstborn—a baby boy named Norman. One-and-a-half years later the sounds became louder still when on October 13, 1957, a baby girl, Iris, was born.

Ernst was gone much of the time, carrying out the responsibilities of three churches, each forty to fifty miles apart. Sigrid never looked back to the comforts she had forfeited, but instead committed herself to building the home and family of the man to whom she had dedicated her life. Convinced she had been called to be the wife of a missionary, she poured herself into that role. When Ernst was home, Sigrid always made sure the children understood his place as head of the household.

By that time six years had passed. The three churches were small but strong. It was time for furlough. Strangely enough, as the Vatters returned to Germany for one year, Ernst's skin had turned mysteriously tan.

CHAPTER TWENTY-FOUR

Death on the Horizon

I t was a cold October day in 1958 when Ernst, Sigrid and their son and daughter exited the train in Germany and made their way to Goenningen. During their time in Japan, Ernst had received the sad news of his uncle's death. He was anxious to comfort Aunt Sofie and see his family again.

While standing in the village bakery eyeing a large block of cheese and smelling the rich aroma of bread, they met Martin Schule, son of Ernst's hometown pastor.

"Ernst! Sigrid! What a pleasant surprise to see you. And look at that tan, Ernst. How did that happen in the middle of winter?"

"I don't know. My skin turned this color before I left Japan."

"I've heard good things about your ministry, that you planted three churches."

"Yes, it's true."

"Ernst, listen. We need someone like you here in Germany. I can assure you that you would soon have a favorable position in the Protestant church. Look at the good you could do."

"Ahhh, that sounds inviting, Martin. Sigrid and I will discuss it, and perhaps we can talk before I leave the village."

"It's a deal. Day after tomorrow at 2 o'clock. Let's meet right here for coffee and apple pie."

"We'll be here."

Ernst and Sigrid walked toward his aunt's home with a block of cheese and a cake. Sigrid was unusually quiet. That night, when they had gone to bed, she finally spoke.

"Ernst! What is there to discuss with Martin? The Lord has called us to Japan. Why didn't you make that clear?"

"Because I'm disgusted. I am strongly considering quitting the Liebenzell Mission."

"What? Why?"

"Well, first there is Mr. Ettling. I appreciate his fine disposition and disciplined ways, but he is not the right leader for Japan. He is suitable for his former work in China, but he has no feel or vision for Japan. Every time I have a plan, he has a problem. Nothing ever gets done."

The terseness in his voice increased. "Then there is the mission itself. It's too far away from the field. The directors simply leave us alone and have no idea what is taking place or how to help us. I can assure you that most of my ideas have found their way into the garbage can. I'm not getting the support and direction that I need. When I pose questions to them, they say, 'Pray, believe God and make your own decision.' While they offer good prayer and financial support, I don't find them giving adequate practical support."

"You know, Ernst, that you are quick in mind and impulsive in action. Perhaps the Lord is using them to slow you down."

Anger arched across his brow as he snapped back. "I'm thoroughly disgusted and am going to think about Martin's offer."

"That's foolish!" Sigrid responded.

"Perhaps. Let's sleep on it," Ernst concluded.

"Fine, but you had better pray long and hard about this. It's serious to back away from God's call," Sigrid persisted.

Two days later, they met Martin.

"Good coffee. We don't get coffee this rich in Japan."

Martin made a sipping sound, then asked, "So, what do you think? Shall I contact people in the church to get things moving?"

Before Ernst could speak, Sigrid leveled her eyes toward Martin's and unflinchingly declared, "This reminds me of the temptation of Jesus—an offer of easy solutions for hard times. Satan promised, 'All this I will give you . . . if you will bow down and worship me' (Matthew 4:9). Jesus replied, 'Worship the Lord your God, and serve him only' (4:10). God has clearly called Ernst to Japan with the Liebenzell Mission, and I don't think he should turn to the right or the left, but continue serving where he is called."

Ernst gulped heavily. Martin looked at Sigrid, hoping to see her grinning, but her expression was cobra cold—a dead serious stare. Martin wiped his mouth, adjusted his posture, cleared his throat and asked, "How do you feel about this, Ernst?"

"My wife is wise. I must slow down and think about these things."

It took a while for winter to thaw as Ernst wrestled with what to do. He was strongly motivated—a man of action—often feeling suffocated by the shop-worn response from his leaders: "You must wait on the Lord." *Wait!* Ernst thought. *Waiting is all those people ever seem to do.* He was hotly driven to *go*, not wait—just as the Great Commission commanded.

One day Sigrid advised, "Ernst, you're always in a rush. Even Moses had to wait when the pillar stopped moving in the desert. Maybe God says, 'Wait, don't work for Me just now. I must first work in you. And I can only do that as you wait before Me.' "

"I know, I know, but it irritates me to waste time talking rather than doing the job."

"But Ernst, you act as though you can do God's work *for* Him. It is He who must do His works: first *in*, then *through* you. Remember, in John 15:5, Jesus said, 'Apart from me you can do nothing.' What you could never do in a lifetime *for* God, He could do in a day *through* you. So maybe it's important to slow down, wait on God and prepare to do greater things by *His* power."

Ernst grunted in begrudging agreement. He knew she was right, but it was hard for him to hear it. His anger was rooted in impatience, so Sigrid's wisdom found limited acceptance.

Outside, the sun was warming the soil. Underground, seeds were bursting open and thrusting upward to carpet the spring floor with a spray of color. The smell of blossoms wafted on mellow breezes, refreshing the air. Ernst, however, could not see the message in this: *Life germinates from death, and everything grows in its proper time.* He was too focused on what had not been accomplished.

But God was still working on him.

"Good morning, Ernst," Sigrid said in a musical tone one day. "Come, enjoy your breakfast."

"This looks good," Ernst said as he bit into a slice of freshly baked bread covered with butter and jam. After a hearty meal of eggs, bacon, fruit and coffee, he sat staring.

"What's on your mind, Ernst?"

"It's not what's on my mind, but what's on my stomach. I don't feel well."

Suddenly, he rose and rushed to the bathroom where he vomited violently.

Sigrid followed him. "What's wrong?" she asked.

"I don't know. I've been feeling weak for days. In fact, I had to force myself to eat this morning. I've been losing my appetite lately."

"You should see a doctor."

"No, no, it's nothing. It will pass, don't worry."

Sigrid put her hand to her mouth but said nothing. Her concern deepened as she saw him grow weaker, eating less and less over the following weeks. His tan was turning ashen.

Finally, one day late in July, Ernst was called to the mission headquarters. While getting out of the car, his knees buckled and he fell to the road. Grabbing the door to pull himself to his feet, he clung there, breathing heavily. Slowly he made his way into the office of Pastor Rommel, the dean.

"Ernst, sit down," said Rommel. "I saw you fall by your car just now. Sigrid has been telling me of your worsening condition. I am asking you—no, ordering you—in all love and respect to visit the Private Hospital for a complete exam. Don't worry, the mission will pay for everything."

On August 10, 1959, Ernst was admitted. By that time he was profoundly weak, though he still made light of it. Following several days of tests, Dr. Neumann entered Ernst's room to present the results. "We've tested you for a tumor on both the liver and the brain. There's nothing in your head. . . ."

"That's what everyone tells me," Ernst jested.

Dr. Neumann barely grinned as he soberly continued. "There's nothing on your liver, at least nothing that we can see. We have no idea what is wrong with you, but we need to try something. I'm going to give you some medicine to see if it helps."

Weeks passed. Even in the hospital, Ernst kept losing his food and growing weaker. His flesh shrank, much as it had in the prison camp, and his face hollowed. His skin color darkened to charcoal gray. Sigrid, who never missed a day visiting her husband, was exceptionally quiet one morning.

"What's wrong, Sigrid?" queried Ernst.

"I have bad news."

"What is it?"

"Your mother passed away suddenly from a stroke."

"She was only sixty."

"I know. But they said it was sudden and painless."

"It's terrible that I cannot even attend my own mother's funeral."

"I understand," said Sigrid as she placed her hand on his.

Ernst's mood became sullen as he walked through memories: his mother's warm spirit that had kept her singing even amid disappointment and pain. The way she made him laugh as a child. Her unconditional acceptance of him at home, and her kind heart, allowing Sofie to raise him. The tears of joy when he returned frail but safe from the prison encampment. Her pride mingled with pain at the dedication service when he was commissioned for Japan; it was his sole memory of her attending the church that sat only a five-minute walk from their home. He could think of no time when she spoke of trusting Christ for her salvation. He could only lie in the sterile hospital room hoping that she had a private trust in the Lord.

The next day, Dr. Neumann entered Ernst's room and somberly stood by his bed, seeking for the right words. The silence was broken, however, by Ernst's impetuous words: "I know I'm going to die."

Startled, Sigrid, who was sitting by his bed, looked up.

"I don't know about that," said Dr. Neumann, "but I'm moving you to the Tropenheim in Tuebingen where they treat tropical diseases. Perhaps you caught something in Japan that we cannot diagnose."

"Tropen nothing. I feel so tired. I will go home to die."

"No, Ernst, don't be foolish. We must not give up hope. We must try everything there is to do," pleaded Sigrid.

"No, I will go home to die," Ernst replied, forgetting the strength of Sigrid's determination.

"Doctor, may I speak with you in the hall?" asked Sigrid.

As they spoke, death was crossing the horizon . . . grim, dark, morbid.

CHAPTER TWENTY-FIVE

Death at the Window

O n September 1, 1959, Ernst was admitted to the Tropenheim. "We're going to run many blood tests, Mr. Vatter," the doctor told him.

"OK, but I feel as though I'm sliding steadily downhill. I feel weaker every day."

Staff doctors began conferring around Ernst's bed almost daily. "We're rapidly running out of things to test, Ernst," the head of the team said to him one day. "We have run additional tests on your brain and can find nothing wrong. We have run more tests on your liver. Nothing. We even had a consulting surgeon from the University Hospital run tests on your stomach, thinking perhaps there might be a tumor. Nothing."

"I guess we can pray," Ernst said. The doctors nodded, more to appease him than to reveal personal faith.

Days passed. Sigrid never failed to appear in the door, flashing her beautiful smile—flooding the room with hope. She never told Ernst that a Scripture had been impressed upon her heart, a promise that she believed was from God. It was printed on a card someone had sent to Ernst which hung on the wall at the foot of his bed. It read: "I will not die but live, and will proclaim what the LORD has done (Psalm 118:17)." This became a witness in her heart that Ernst would be healed, though that rope of faith would soon unravel and fray to a single strand, seemingly too thin to hold Ernst from dropping to the bottom of the valley of death.

Ernst, on the other hand, found himself unsettled about the prospect of soon being in the presence of the Lord. His thoughts became dark and heavy, filled with conviction. One day, when all alone, he lifted his weakening voice to God:

> I can see that much of my service to You was pride-based. I wasn't trying to earn salvation by my works, but I acted as though I could do Your work for You. Now I see that only You can do Your own work. I was not a yielded vessel to be used at Your discretion. I was harsh with people who didn't work hard enough, or who didn't do things my way. I have been completely egocentric. Now, I am soon going to be in Your presence, and I feel as though I have nothing to give You.
>
> I see more clearly than ever that all of salvation—and all of service—is based upon Your grace and mercy. I'm asking for Your forgiveness for the selfish manner in which I tried to do Your work. How I wish I had another chance to live the things I have learned while lying upon this bed. But it seems to be too late for that. . . .

Although he felt secure in his salvation, day after day Ernst lifted this prayer to God, remorseful that his service had been done in his own strength. He had understood grace for salvation; he was now learning it for service too. But with each day death edged closer to his window.

Just one week after his mother's death, Sigrid entered his room with another announcement. "Ernst, there is a reason why your father has not come to see you."

"What is it?"

"He's being treated for cancer at the University Hospital."

"It's all happening at once: first me, then Mother, now Dad."

"It's all such a mystery," Sigrid agreed. "We can only trust God's wisdom. I'm praying, Ernst, that this burden will not discourage you in your own fight."

As the valley of personal loss deepened, Ernst spent his days thinking through the ultimate questions of life, reaching for the values that last forever. But it seemed so late. Why hadn't he learned these things when he had health and life with which to serve? Another week of physical suffering and spiritual anguish passed.

On September 21 Sigrid brightened the room once again with her warm singsong greeting, though it had grown harder to be positive at the sight of Ernst's frail form. But this day, after much thought, Ernst was ready to face death head-on.

"Hello, Sigrid. Please, come sit. I must speak with you about some matters."

Sigrid sat lightly on the chair by the bed and took Ernst's hand. The tendons felt fragile enough to snap. She thought to herself, *My husband is going to die, just as his mother did only a few weeks ago.*

He startled her by echoing her thoughts. "Sigrid, I'm going to die."

She put two fingers against his lips to hush him. She was tired, both in body and spirit, from caring for their son and daughter, plus Ernst's aged Aunt Sofie—all while watching the life drain from her husband. Such words seemed too heavy for her now.

He gently moved her fingers aside and continued. "I love you and do not want to say these things, but we must talk about my funeral."

"Yes, all right," she said in a half whisper. The other men in the room lay motionless, their eyes riveted on the ceiling.

"I must talk about this now, as I am losing my ability to collect my thoughts. I can't pray anymore. I have no control over my mind."

"I understand. Let's talk."

"I would like Pastor Hertel to speak at the service. As the Liebenzell Overseas Director he will best represent what I want to say. Please tell him to emphasize the mercy and grace of God. That is what saved me from the world and enabled us to serve in Japan."

Finding it hard to go on, Sigrid squeezed his hand.

He looked at her only to see tears flowing freely from her eyes. "I'm sorry, Sigrid."

"Oh, Ernst, we formed such wonderful dreams sitting on our bench in Japan. This was certainly not part of our dreams, was it? This is so hard. . . ."

Ernst drew in a deep breath, then released an involuntary sob. After collecting himself, he continued, "I would like to have 'What a Friend We Have in Jesus' sung. I like that hymn. He has been a wonderful friend to me. He never threw me away when I blundered."

"It will be as you desire."

"I want you to marry again . . ."

"Ernst!"

"No, it's OK, you must. I don't want you and the children to be alone. You're a wonderful wife. It is only right that you remarry with my blessing."

Sigrid sobbed openly. The other men in the room barely breathed. Ernst cleared his throat from the choke hold of sorrow.

"Sigrid, my dear, I only have one final request." The word "final" cut into her heart afresh. She nodded for him to continue. "When you remarry, please allow our son to bear my last name. I want my family name preserved through him."

"Of course, Ernst, of course," she whispered.

The room was respectfully silent as they sat together into the late afternoon. Sigrid tenderly brushed her husband's face, sometimes wiping away a fresh stream of tears. They held hands: clutching the moment, clinging to life, occasionally whispering kind words of love and encouragement. Their dreams had surrendered to the reality of approaching death. Finally, the inevitable moment of departure came. Sigrid reluctantly rose and said, "I'll be back tomorrow."

"No, please sit beside me longer."

"I want to, but I can't. I must tend to the children and Aunt Sofie."

"I'm sorry, I know you must go. I love you. I will look forward to seeing you tomorrow. Come as early as you can."

She kissed him, walked to the door, turned and waved good-bye. He lifted several fingers in response. Then the doorway was empty—unbearably empty. Ernst listened until he could hear her footsteps no more.

Back home at Aunt Sofie's, Sigrid lost coordination between her mind, her body and her faith. All three seemed to be flying in random directions. Her body quaked, her thoughts spun and her faith waned. She wept uncontrollably. Despair was closer than air. Finally, she dropped to her knees and cried out, "Oh, God, my nerves cannot handle this anymore! I have our children, along with Ernst's aunt, to care for. I'm torn between the need to fulfill my responsibilities and wanting to be with Ernst. The thought of losing him is too much right now. All of life is unraveling around me, and You seem so distant. I desire to trust You and honor You in the middle of this trouble, but I can do no more except surrender Ernst to You. If You want to take him home, then so be it."

It felt as though someone had opened a window; she felt a breeze of hope drive away the despair. It wasn't hope that he'd live, but that God would not abandon her. She realized that the enemy had pounced upon her natural need for security as well as her love for Ernst. When both were entrusted to God, a peace that could not be explained took command of her heart.

Back at the hospital, Ernst looked at a scrap of paper that a minister friend had taped to the wall at the foot of his bed. Taken from Jeremiah 31:3 it read, "I have loved you with an everlasting love." The message penetrated Ernst's heart in an unusual way. He squinted as a darkness marched toward his eyes, a strange occurrence since the horizon was still aglow.

Ernst struggled to mouth the words, "I . . . I have . . . I have loved . . . I have loved you . . ." His mouth felt thick and cottony as he wrapped his lips around the words. The harder he tried to force the words out, the more they eluded him. A creeping numbness engulfed his body. The darkness drew closer until there was no more than a small shaft of light left, through which he could see the verse on the wall. Then that, too, narrowed and closed—and all went black. Ernst had lapsed into unconsciousness, sliding deeper and deeper until reaching bottom.

"Mr. Vatter . . . Mr. Vatter?" No response. The nurse's voice became louder as she sought to rouse him. She patted his arm. "Mr. Vatter!" Nothing. "Oh, my," she said, and rushed for a doctor. The doctor came to his bedside and opened Ernst's eyelids to find that his eyes were staring ahead, zombie straight.

"Coma. He's in the final throes of dying," said the doctor. "It could be hours, it could be days, but he's going to die. Put him in the dying room." Then he left. The dying room was exactly that, a place where they put people to die in private dignity.

The nurse was not a large woman and no gurneys were available, so she got another nurse to help her move Ernst's body. Though frail, his frame was still too heavy for them. "Oh!" they both exclaimed as he slipped from their grasp and fell between them to the floor. Both felt sickened, though they knew Ernst had felt nothing.

One of the men in the room got out of bed and said, "I know this man. Please, let me help you." Ernst's arms and legs dangled limply as the roommate carried him to the solitary room of the inevitable and gently placed him on a bed. The nurses compassionately tucked a blanket around him. Death edged from the window to his bedside.

Sigrid, knowing none of this, had dropped into a deep sleep. A call from the hospital jolted her awake.

"Mrs. Vatter, this is the head nurse. Shortly after you left last evening your husband slipped into a coma. The doctor is certain his time is short. This is the final stage. You must hurry if you want to be with him while he is yet alive. Be assured we are giving him the best possible care."

"Thank you. I'll be right there," Sigrid replied softly. She pressed one hand against her stomach as she cradled the receiver.

Was last night our last good-bye? she wondered. *Did I misunderstand the verse about his deliverance, or was God only assuring me that Ernst will be in the resurrection?* Her body and mind could take no more. She forced herself to rush, though mindlessly, in order to see her Ernst one more time. Just before she left the house she called the Liebenzell Mission.

"Pastor Achenbach, Ernst is dying. They are sure it will be soon. Would you have the college staff pray?"

"Yes, Mrs. Vatter. I'll call churches and ask them to pray as well. How is your faith holding up?"

"It faces turmoil," Sigrid replied honestly. "I believe God gave me a Scripture that Ernst will live, that this illness is meant to glorify God. Now it appears hopeless. In my heart I have peace, but my mind gets confused when circumstances fly out of control. Keeping my mind and my heart joined in peace is not easy."

"Just know that it's not unusual for the heart to know peace while the mind is troubled. But we'll continue believing God. Perhaps He still has a miracle for us."

"Yes, perhaps He does," she heard herself replying, then hung up.

Pastor Achenbach canceled all classes that day and assembled everyone to pray for the dying missionary. He also called Rev. Hertel and asked him to go to the hospital to comfort Sigrid.

As Sigrid drove from Goenningen to Tuebingen, her foot was pressed down upon the gas pedal and her heart was lifted up to the Lord. "Jesus, You gave me that verse, that hope. Now it's Your turn to act!"

Ernst was deep in a coma. His liver could no longer cleanse his body of poison. Lethal toxins coursed through his veins with each heartbeat. Despite his unconscious state, the poisons in his brain occasionally caused his body to thrash in convulsions. It looked cruel, but his hands and feet had to be tied to the bed so that his involuntary movements would not send him crashing to the floor. Filled with both sorrow and hope, Sigrid entered the hospital where the doctor was waiting to see her.

"Mrs. Vatter, I assure you that we did all that could be done. However, I must also tell you that the poison has robbed his brain of so much oxygen that should he recover, the brain damage might leave him incompetent. I'm sorry."

Thus, another weight was hung on that last strand of faith. Still, she sweetly responded, "Thank you for being honest, doctor."

"We moved him to a different room last night. He's in there. One more thing . . . at times he thrashes because of the poison in his brain, so we had to tie his hands and feet."

Sigrid stepped to the doorway and saw Ernst tied in a blanket. She clutched her throat and gasped. Reality hit her full force when she realized that her husband was in the dying room. Her heart pounding heavily, she gingerly walked to his side and enfolded his hand in hers. Cool, he felt so cool. Her once vivacious husband was now helpless, dying.

"Dear God," she softly prayed, "men have done their best. Now You must show what only You can do." Ernst lay motionless, only occasionally twitching and thrashing; indeed, a man in the grip of death. But he was her love, not just another man. She heard footsteps shuffling behind her.

"Mother! Father! Thank you for coming." All three embraced.

Clasping her hands in his, Sigrid's father asked, "How are you doing, my dear?" He brushed away new tears from her soft cheek.

"Ernst's sister Hedwig is caring for the children and Aunt Sofie. I do feel the Lord helping me each day, and am certain that even if this is the end, the Lord will go with me. The scripture that comes to my mind many times a day is Psalm 23:4, 'Even though I walk through the valley of the shadow of death, I will fear no evil, for you are with me.' I may have to go on without Ernst, but I won't be alone . . ." She choked back another wave of tears, trying to muster courage. "The Lord will be with me."

Silently, they stood in the supportive strength of mutual faith. Soon another pair of footsteps was heard and Rev. Hertel entered the room.

"Good morning," he said quietly. Then, looking at Sigrid he asked, "Could I be here with you and Ernst alone for a few moments?" Sigrid's parents politely stepped out of the room. Pastor Hertel opened his Bible and read the passage from James about praying for the sick, then he walked to the bed and placed his hands upon Ernst's body.

"Heavenly Father," he prayed aloud, "I am an old man of seventy. My life is behind me. I have served you as best I know how. Ernst here is a young man with his life before him. Please take me, not him. I am willing to pass and go home in his place. I am no longer needed, but he is. He has a wife and two children. He has a life to offer for ministry. Give him back his life and take mine in his place. I pray this in Jesus' name."

Turning to Sigrid, he said, "Be encouraged. We will soon see what the Lord chooses to do." As suddenly as he came he departed, and Sigrid's parents reentered the room.

Death still demanded its prey. Ernst lay suspended in the comatose chasm of nothingness, his chest slowly rising and falling—each time seemed final. Sigrid and her family sat in silence, watching. Her father thought of his strong rebuke toward Ernst for telling Sigrid he wanted a healthy wife, and he remembered telling Ernst that no one could know whose health would suffer. But he never imagined this turn of events.

Soon long evening shadows cast a dim ambiance of finality across the room. Sigrid decided to stay . . . waiting to see what God would do. It was then that a strange event occurred. A young doctor who had just returned from vacation was asked to look at the dying man. When he entered the room and saw Ernst, his eyes grew large. He didn't speak, rather, he yelled.

CHAPTER TWENTY-SIX

The Race Against Death

"What is this man doing in this hospital? He doesn't belong here! Don't you know what he has? He has Addison's disease. Only Dr. Heny at the University Hospital can help him. Get him there now . . . *now*!" His voice echoed through the cavernous halls like an explosion.

One nurse picked up the phone to call for an ambulance. Another ran down the hall to grab a gurney, its wheels racing across the tile floor as the nurse pushed it as fast as she could. The swishing sound of stiff uniforms could be heard rushing in every direction. Sigrid stood back, holding her hand over her mouth, then walked quickly beside Ernst as he was rolled to the ambulance.

Outside, Sigrid's father caught a glimpse of Ernst through the ambulance window—and was amazed to see him smiling!

"Move! Move!" ordered the young doctor. "We have no time left."

There was a jolt, and the ambulance raced into the night, rushing to outpace death. Sigrid followed close behind in her car. Alone, she drove and prayed. "Oh, God, let Your will be done . . ."

Dr. Heny and several nurses were waiting outside the University Hospital as the ambulance came to an abrupt halt. The driver scrambled out, ran to the back and yanked open the door. Hands reached for the gurney and pulled it from the ambulance. Ernst was wheeled into an examination room where Dr. Heny lifted his eyelid.

"Coma. Deep coma," he mumbled, then instinctively followed his training. "Draw blood now. Inject him with cortisone and fluid."

He turned to Sigrid. "Are you his wife?"

"Yes."

"I have no time to explain my procedure. We have only one chance to save him and it's a very small one. I fear, however, that there may be too much brain damage already. If we save him, your husband may be a mentally impaired man the rest of his life."

"I've been told that already, Doctor. Try to save him. There are many people praying."

Dr. Heny turned and focused his total attention on saving his patient. He kept the infusion running. The fluid seeped into Ernst's veins, drop by drop.

Hours later there was no more left to do, except wait—the most difficult task of all. Wait on death? Wait on life? Wait on God.

Sigrid sat on a hard chair in the waiting room. Deep into the night, she was bent over, half asleep. Ernst lay alone in a darkened room. Throughout the night a nurse repeatedly came and went—checking his pulse, the liquid, the cortisone. Green blips steadily appeared and disappeared on a scope, tracing each heartbeat. Two miracles were needed: life and lucidity. Both were improbable. The young wife and mother awaiting her husband's fate awaited her own as well.

Each tick of the large clock on the wall drew her closer and closer to an unalterable future.

The suspense broke just before dawn when Ernst groaned—again and again, louder and louder. The nurse was immediately at his side. Ernst's eyes, barely open, saw what looked like the blurry form of a person amid smoke—a strange moving form. Slowly, he focused and realized it was an elderly nurse. She was bending over him, adjusting tubes and arranging sheets around his body. He knew not that he was ascending the long tunnel of a coma, reemerging into the world he had departed for two days. Then he felt something awful—humiliating. He was completely wet from passing water. "Oh, I'm so embarrassed," he mumbled. "Please forgive me."

The nurse responded in a motherly matter-of-fact tone. "Mr. Vatter, do not mind that. It is what we hoped for. It's your only chance to flush the poisons from your system. It seems to be working; otherwise, you would not be speaking to me right now. Don't you feel embarrassed."

Moments later Doctor Heny entered the room and said, "I can't believe it, but something is going on here. We'll keep the infusion running. There is still little hope, but at least something is happening."

Ernst was now in a deep sleep, but not a coma. At noon he woke up and spoke again.

"Where's my wife? I want to see Sigrid."

Ernst's sister Hedwig had come that morning and was standing by his bed. "Brother, please be quiet. Sigrid is right over there fast asleep. She is terribly exhausted and must get rest."

"I need food. I'm hungry."

Raising clenched hands in salute, the head nurse said, "This is the best news of all. First you are awake, second you are speaking coherently and now you want food. So, food you shall have."

Ernst understood none of the fuss. All he knew was that the prospect of food sounded very good to his awakening appetite.

Ernst was slurping down some soup and bread when Sigrid awoke. She sat straight up in amazement, exclaiming, "Ernst!"

Her husband was restored to life! It felt like a resurrection—*and so it was*! "Let me help you," she said as she rushed to his side and fed him like a mother coddling her child.

As word spread throughout the Liebenzell Mission, prayer turned from petition to praise. Then started weeks of tests and consultations at the hospital. At long last, the day came when Ernst would be released to go home to rest. He entered a room for his last meeting with the doctor before departure.

"Ernst," said Dr. Heny, "you are an amazing case. We are witnessing something unexplainable."

Ernst grinned.

"Well, it's more than surviving the coma that I speak of. Frankly, I was most surprised when you woke up. I don't believe in miracles, but this is the closest to one I have ever come. But, further, the adrenal glands on the top of your kidneys are gone. They do not show up on any X ray. I can only assume that the tuberculosis you had in your lungs moved to your glands and destroyed them. Without those glands, it's impossible to live! We have had lengthy consultations among the medical staff to try to determine how it is that you are alive at all."

"What does all this mean to my future?"

"First, you will have to take cortisone every day for the rest of your life. The cortisone will help balance your system in the absence of the glands. It may produce some undesirable side effects; still, you must take it daily."

"That's no problem. I'm sure I can take the medication with me when I return to Japan."

"No, you don't understand. There will be no more Japan, no more *anyplace*. You will have a problem with profuse sweating. A warmer climate could easily end your life. You must *never* leave Germany!"

"Doctor, I *will* be going to Japan."

"You are foolish!"

"Maybe so, but I am going back to Japan, and I will see you when I return in six years—alive."

"OK, fine," Dr. Heny said to pacify his impossible patient. "But there's more. You will not be able to father any more children. Because you no longer have adrenal glands, you will be sterile."

"Dr. Heny, children come as a gift from the Lord. When I return in six years to show you that I'm alive, I'll also introduce you to my new children."

Dr. Heny gave a pathetic chuckle as he shook his head at the stubborn man who seemingly didn't understand the reality of medical science. "All right, Mr. Vatter, I'll meet your new children," he conceded, feeling sure that Ernst would lose this argument.

On October 28, 1959, Ernst left the hospital to rest at the Tannenhoehe Christian Rest Home in the Black Forest, located near Sigrid's parents' home.

"I feel so sorry for you, Ernst," Sigrid said. "This is a different experience for you, isn't it—waiting and resting, I mean."

"Yes, I'm accustomed to running places, meeting dead-lines and sitting in boring board meetings. But I know that I'm still a sick man. My strength is a long way off. I will use this time to read the Scriptures and pray. As you know, I have always spent time reading and praying every morning, but now I want to spend entire days doing that."

"I think the Lord wants you to know Him better. I believe He is preparing you for something special."

One day some Christian brothers came to visit Ernst. "We want to pray for your complete healing. We believe God does not want you to be sick at all. All we need to do is pray in faith and you will be healed in such a way as to never need medicine again."

So they began to pray, not realizing that faith doesn't awaken God to heal; rather, God awakens faith when He is going to heal. Days went by and no answer came. One morning Ernst was walking through the Black Forest with his Bible and came to a clearing. He sat down on a fallen log amid the rich smell of pine. Birds swooped from tree to tree, sometimes squabbling, sometimes calling to mates. Squirrels chattered as they scampered about, hiding nuts and chasing each other in playful circles around tree trunks. A hawk drifted lazily above looking for a meal.

Ernst, opening his Bible to Second Corinthians 12:7, came upon the words God spoke to Paul about his "thorn in [the] flesh." He read that God chose not to deliver Paul, but rather said, "My grace is sufficient for you" (12:9). The words exploded in his heart as though meant specifically for him. It is rare that a person hears God's voice, but when it happens it's unmistakable. Ernst heard no audible voice, just a deep impression coupled with a complete peace. He knew it was from the Lord's.

Days later the men returned to continue praying for Ernst's healing. "No," said Ernst, "we will no longer pray this way. Thank you so much for your concern, but the Lord has shown me clearly that this problem is here to teach me humility and dependence upon Him. Otherwise, I know that my self-confidence will lead me astray. Living with this illness will certainly keep me close to the Lord."

"Ernst, this is nonsense," they remonstrated.

"The doctor thinks I am foolish for saying that I'll return to Japan and have more children. You think I'm unwise for not wanting you to pray for my healing anymore. But something is happening inside of my heart that is greater than a complete healing of my body. Sigrid believes God is preparing me to be used in some way.

"After the war I established Jesus Christ as the Savior and Lord of my life. I confronted my anger by learning to walk in the Spirit and not the flesh. Now I'm learning dependence upon God for my very next breath. I'm beginning to understand that breath itself is sustained by God, not merely natural causes. My personality hasn't changed, but something deep within me is changing. And that change will not be complete without my having to look to God daily for my very survival."

One afternoon, as Sigrid and Ernst sat together on a windswept hill overlooking a dark valley thick with pines, Sigrid spoke, saying, "I overheard you telling Dr. Heny at the hospital that you were going back to Japan. So, you have changed your mind about leaving the mission?"

"Yes, I have. Through this illness God has shown me many things about myself, things I don't like to see, but they are true. I was serving God in my own strength. I thought when I saw something that needed to be done that it was my role to get it done, even if it meant being harsh with people who seemed lazy. I now realize that people, not projects, must come first. In fact, I just bought a desktop sign that reads: 'People Before Projects.'

"Also, I have been overwhelmed by the love given to me from the people of the Liebenzell Mission. I can see now that they were doing their best for us in the field, which is all I have a right to expect. My critical spirit made me demanding of them and blinded me from trusting the Lord. I must look to God and not man for my supply. That became clear when no doctor on earth could save me. If God could save me from the jaws of death, He can also supply all our needs in the field, even when the mission can't."

Sigrid smiled. "I'm pleased to hear that. I think this is part of what the Lord has been after."

Ernst continued, "Life is made of radical experiences followed by the process of living out the lessons learned, and that is never easy. I feel much like Lazarus. First, Jesus called him from the grave, then he told the disciples to unwrap his grave clothes. After that he still had to live out a life of faithful obedience to God, facing pressures, problems and temptations like everyone else."

"So, what you're saying is that you have also been called back from death . . . like Lazarus. Now you have to live out your miracle in a practical life of obedience."

"Yes. As Lazarus' story spread, he drew large crowds, then Jesus would preach to them. I wonder how God will use this event in my life to glorify Himself and fulfill His purpose."

"I wonder about that too. I'm sure the Lord will reveal that in His time," Sigrid responded.

"That's true. But I feel as though I have a lot of grave clothes yet to be unwrapped. It's one thing to be drawn back from the grave, but another thing altogether to shed all the grave clothes. That always takes time."

"Yes, then we'll see how God wants to use this miracle."

On March 26, 1960, Ernst and Sigrid departed for Japan for their second six-year term. After disembarking from the ship, they boarded a train that steamed and chugged toward the mission station of Nakanoshima. The shrill whistle screamed and the wheels clicked and clacked as the train roared past the Todai Station.

"There! Look, Sigrid. It's *our* bench. It looks so lonely."

CHAPTER TWENTY-SEVEN

Life After the Miracle

Sigrid looked at the man whom she had nearly lost and lay her hand on his. He smiled, squeezed her hand and said, "It's good to be back." He looked back as the train sped past "their" bench and watched it recede further into their past. Then, after a moment of deep reflection, he looked at Sigrid and repeated, "It's *really* good to be back. I feel as though I'm starting life all over again. Every day is freshly new and filled with hope."

"Yes, but this time you have the advantage of the wisdom gained from your experience."

"That's true. It's amazing how God must take us through such deep problems in order to get what we know in our heads into the control center of our hearts."

"What do you think is the most important thing you learned through your illness?"

"First, I have learned that both life and death are in God's hands. Second, I have a deeper awareness that nothing is accomplished in life—from breathing to preaching—apart from the strength of the Lord. And third, I must not seek God to bless *my* plans. Rather, I must seek Him for the daily power and direction to fulfill *His* plans."

Soon they arrived at their destination. Ernst's appointment to replace Rev. Ettling as field director for Japan found them unpacking and setting up home at Nakano-shima.

"I will see you less than ever now that you are the field director," Sigrid said as they made a special place for the 3,000 cortisone tablets which were as essential to Ernst's liver as air to his lungs. "My only concern is that the children will also see less of their father than before. Time with Papa is a precious commodity."

"No, I have a plan. I expect to be home for lunch most days. It's my evenings that will be busy. So everyday after lunch I want to have one hour alone with the children. I want them to know they have a dad who cares."

The first day of "Dad's time" frightened Sigrid. Arriving home early from the market, she heard laughing, screaming and thumping—a ruckus that had the entire neighborhood wondering what was happening in the Vatter household. She opened the door and saw Ernst spinning like a merry-go-round with one child under each arm.

"Ernst! You're much too rough."

"Stay out of the way or I'll spin you, too!" he managed to puff out. His eyes were wide with excitement. Dignity had to wait outside. He had plunged wholeheartedly into his children's world.

Sigrid muttered as she went to the kitchen, but couldn't help imagining what it would feel like to be spun.

*　*　*

Not long after accepting his position, Ernst walked directly into the wall of resistance that often awaits new leadership—those who wanted to challenge his authority.

"There's a lot of talk about you among the missionaries," confided one of the men.

"What are they saying?"

"Although you have been in this field longer than any other, some say you are not competent. Others are irritated by your personality: Some say you're too strict, others think you're too decisive, while still others grumble about your straightforwardness, saying you act too forcefully."

Ernst put his hand to his chin and looked beyond the horizon, remembering his own criticisms of Rev. Ettling and of the mission.

Finally, after a few long, awkward moments, the young missionary added, "I hope I did the right thing by coming to you about this. I don't want to cause trouble but thought you should know."

"My good man, you're not stirring trouble. I shall seek the best way to mature from your words."

After the young man departed, Ernst returned to deep contemplation. *Where are the old feelings?* he wondered. *Where is the anger that would have once caused me to react harshly? What is this new desire to genuinely learn from these criticisms? Anger and defensiveness once fatigued me. By accepting these criticisms as a means for growth, I find strength in my spirit.*

That evening he told Sigrid about his experience.

"Much of what the missionary said to you is true, Ernst," she said kindly. "You really don't listen to what people are saying. I think that makes them feel frustrated and insignificant, and underlies much of their opposition."

"Before, when people exposed my sinfulness, I exploded in self-defense. Now I welcome their words. They help me to see where I yet need to seek God's help to grow."

Sigrid got up from the table to take some dishes to the kitchen. As she did, he heard her voice trailing off, "Ernst,

I married the right man. Only a man after God's own heart talks like this."

But Ernst's inner world was not all that was changing. On April 23, 1961, he found himself in the same hospital where his first two children were born. Now, his third was soon to be delivered.

"Dr. Eitel, I want to be present when my third child is born. I want to be with Sigrid."

"Forbidden. I never allow husbands in the room. I have enough trouble without a fainting husband dropping on the floor."

Ernst realized that this rigid, straightforward German doctor was not going to yield, so he backed down. Once again, he was struck by the fact that the old Ernst, who would have plowed into this doctor with a verbal assault, was silent—peacefully silent. All he did was enjoy the sound of the new baby's name—Anette.

On March 28, 1964, he was back at the hospital for Evelyne's birth, their fourth child. This time, as the doctor walked by and pointed to the waiting room, Ernst just smiled, sat down and waited.

For Ernst, a huge example of the change taking place within him came the night he returned home from a trip at 3 in the morning and found Sigrid sitting at the table crying.

"What's wrong?"

"I let the cat out hours ago and it hasn't returned."

Ernst did not feel the urge to laugh as he would have when seeing things only from his own perspective. Since he did not care for cats, he would have at one time viewed her tears as silly. He was as surprised as Sigrid when he heard himself say, "Let's pray for the cat." They did.

As soon as Ernst closed the prayer, he went to the window and there sat the cat waiting to get in. "Look, God has answered already." Ernst placed the cat in Sigrid's arms. He didn't care for the cat one bit more than before, but felt fulfilled to see Sigrid so full of joy.

"Sigrid," he said, "I am truly amazed at the work God is doing to change my heart. But I must say that the greater miracle is that you never got bitter toward me despite my past attitudes."

"God has been good to both of us, Ernst. There's no place for bitterness. We are both changing, and that is what matters the most."

CHAPTER TWENTY-EIGHT

Return of the Death Angel

I t was hot—August hot!—when their second six-year term drew to a close. Ernst and Sigrid took their four children on vacation in Karuizawa, a scenic retreat for missionaries. There was only one interruption to their relaxation . . .

"Sigrid, today I must go down to Tokyo in order to preach. I'll return late tomorrow. Then the rest of the time is ours to enjoy."

"That's fine. I'll be praying for you."

Soon Ernst was gone, and the day wore on as Sigrid invented ways to keep the widely varied interests of the children occupied. The next afternoon life took a sharp turn for the worse when Evelyne, sixteen months old, burst out crying. She stood stiff from shock under the big walnut tree where she had been playing. Fear filled her eyes as she screamed loudly.

Sigrid rushed over and gathered her into her arms, wondering what was wrong. But the child just cried, struggling for breath. Marianne, a neighbor, heard Sigrid's concerned voice and rushed to her side. Opening Evelyne's mouth, she discovered a green kernel, bitten and oozing white fluid. Marianne removed the kernel, carefully tasted a tiny drop, then quickly spit it out.

"My dear, that's hot like fire! It's burning her mouth and throat."

Under the tree in the once peaceful garden, they found the plant among some of Evelyne's toys. Only later were they told that in times past the plant had been used to make poison darts for bear hunting.

"Honey, were you playing with this . . .?"

Evelyne timidly nodded her head.

Not wanting to further frighten the child, Marianne said as calmly as possible, "This must be a very dangerous plant. We need to get her to the hospital immediately."

By that time the commotion had attracted the attention of a fellow missionary who offered to transport Sigrid and Evelyne. The car sped. The hospital doors were flung open. A Japanese doctor greeted them.

"My daughter chewed a plant. It must have been poisonous. Now she can't swallow and can barely breathe." By that time, Evelyne's face was ashen.

"I must perform a tracheotomy immediately or the child will suffocate. There are no nurses to help."

"Operate!" Sigrid said without flinching. "I will hold her."

The doctor looked at her with disbelief, ready to tell her he didn't think she could handle the sight. Sigrid drew her daughter's limp body tightly to her own and gave the doctor a look that was like a command to act. After Evelyne slipped into unconsciousness, the doctor took a sharp knife, lanced the little one's windpipe and slid a tube into the opening.

"There's nothing more I can do, Mrs. Vatter. You can use this room. All we can do is wait."

"What are her chances, Doctor?"

"Not good. The poison is in her system, her throat is swollen and there is a mass of burnt tissue. So we must hope that her body will tolerate the poison until it is out of her, the swelling goes down and she coughs out the damaged tissue. In fairness, however, I must tell you that I see little hope." With that, the doctor departed.

Sigrid lay her little girl on the bed, stroked her clammy brow and prayed. Intent, she never noticed the room turn shadowy, then dark as the day slipped away. Deep into the evening she threw a blanket on the floor beside Evelyne's bed. Then she lay down and draped an arm on the bed, never losing touch with her daughter.

It was close to midnight when Ernst returned to their cabin and felt the darkness. He wondered why Sigrid had not left a light on for him. As he jangled the keys to open the door, he was startled by the sound of Marianne's voice.

"Ernst!"

"Oh, my, what are you doing out so late?"

"Ernst, little Evelyne ate a poisonous plant today."

"What?" Ernst responded with a look of horror.

"Yes, it's true. Hans Menzel went to the hospital with Sigrid and Evelyne. They are still there. The rest of the children are at my house."

Ernst bolted to his car, his neighbor's voice fading behind him, "Please be careful." The car shook and the wheels screeched as he ripped through the night toward the hospital. He jumped out of the car, leaving it parked askew, slammed the unlocked door and ran into the hospital. He entered Evelyne's room fearing the worse. In the dim light he saw his daughter lying still on the bed and his wife on the floor.

"Sigrid?" he whispered, gently brushing her brow. She roused.

"Oh, Ernst, I'm so glad you're finally here."

"How is she?"

"It's not good, Ernst. You must pray. She's getting worse. There is burnt tissue and swelling blocking her breathing and the poison is still in her. If she can't expel the poison and the tissue, she will die. Her little body is fighting, but she's very weak. There is no hope apart from the Lord."

Ernst felt all of his strength drain onto the floor. "I will talk with the doctor," he said, his voice shaking. His hand trembled as he turned the doorknob and quietly departed the room. He found the doctor in the hallway.

"I'm Ernst Vatter. That's my daughter in there. Can anything more be done?"

"No. We can only wait. I know it's hard. I wish I could give you hope."

Ernst then phoned their German doctor, who was aware of the situation. "Doctor Eitel, is there anything more that can be done for my daughter?"

"I must be honest with you, Ernst, nothing can be done just now. But there's an American pediatrician in Karuizawa; I'll inform him. And we will pray for all of you."

Discouraged, Ernst left the hospital and returned home to see his other children. He also needed sleep, but found the horrors of hell awaited him. The Accuser's voice was almost audible as it screamed, "Fool! Why did you go away to preach? If only you'd been home you could have prevented this. Now you'll lose your daughter, all because you had to go and preach." The night was alive with condemnation. He knew it wasn't true, but felt the sting of the accusations all the same.

In his mind he envisioned Evelyne's bright face looking up, worshiping him as her childhood hero. He imagined her tiny hands stretched upward to be lifted into his strong arms. Hot tears flowed down his cheeks when he realized that he might never see her smiling at him again. He prayed it would not be so.

Sigrid didn't sleep either. Back in the hospital she held an oxygen hose over her daughter's throat and listened to the little girl breathing through the tube. By mid-afternoon, Evelyne's breathing was labored and her tiny chest rose and fell with great effort to gain the smallest amount of air. Frightened, Sigrid called for the doctor who at once pulled out the tube that had become blocked with sticky tissue. Evelyne's breath then flowed freely.

Word of the crisis had spread among the missionaries and throughout the town. German, British and American missionaries gathered to pray. Ernst went to join the group but was barely able to speak. Someone asked, "How is your baby girl?" He started to answer, but found the words stuck in his throat. He stretched his chin upward as if to free them, but they wouldn't dislodge. Then he dropped his head into his hands and wept uncontrollably.

"We understand," said one missionary, placing his arm across Ernst's shoulders. "Please, Ernst, go to your children, and we'll pray. I don't think you can help us here."

Ernst spent the next two hours at home, trying to keep the children—and his thoughts—distracted. Finally, he mustered the strength to return to the hospital. Nearing the room he was numbed by the silence, which served to confirm his fear. He saw Sigrid sitting motionless by the bed. His daughter lay still. *It's over. My baby's gone*, he thought.

"Mr. Vatter," said the doctor as he briskly rounded the corner, slightly bumping Ernst's arm. "I'm glad you're back. I have good news. The child brought up all the burnt tissue a short time ago. She coughed it out, and now she's breathing comfortably."

Ernst's jaw hung loosely as he whispered, "Thank the Lord." He felt an infusion of strength warming him. Sigrid hadn't noticed him until she heard the doctor's voice. Looking up, she beamed. Their eyes met in oneness. Words were unnecessary. They had crossed another bridge of crisis together and found their hearts intimately blended more deeply than ever. Ernst departed to tell—no, shout!—the news to the missionaries who were praying.

For two weeks fellow missionaries did housework and brought food to Ernst and the children at home, while they encouraged Sigrid and Evelyne in the hospital. Often, throughout that time and the months that followed, Ernst looked at his friends with a mixture of admiration and guilt: admiration for their tireless love, and guilt for the critical spirit he had toward some of them in the past if they didn't measure up to his work expectations. Again, he was learning that Christianity is about people, not programs. He took another giant step toward seeing the higher value in relationship over productivity.

* * *

On May 2, 1966, the family stepped back on German soil to begin their second furlough. Ernst immediately arranged to see Dr. Heny at the University Hospital in Tuebingen.

"Good morning, Mr. Vatter. I remember you well. I still find it hard to believe that you're alive. Anyway, it's good to see you."

"Thank you," Ernst said with a smile like a banner. "We just arrived back from our six-year stint in Japan, and I wanted to see you. I deeply appreciate all that you've done."

"So, you really did defy my words and go to Japan?"

"Yes, we went to Japan, not in defiance of you, but in obedience to God."

"You obviously made it, and quite well at that."

"Yes, but there's more. Do you remember telling me that I would never be able to father more children?" Ernst asked, handing the doctor a few family photographs.

"Yes, medically that would be impossible."

"Well, we had two children when we left for Japan—Norman and Iris. But do you see these other two in the photographs? You can see by their ages that they were born since I left here. This is Anette, who was born in 1961, and Evelyne, who was born in 1964."

"You're not their father," Dr. Heny replied with a mischievous grin.

"Look closely," said Ernst.

"Yes, I can't deny that they look like you." The doctor put his hand to his chin and slowly shook his head, unwilling to concede to another miracle, yet unable to deny the evidence.

Toward the end of the year's furlough, Ernst went to the top of "fire mountain" to be alone, searching for some understanding. The panoramic setting was always electrifying: the steeply sloped funnel to the town of Liebenzell, the large chalet-style buildings perched on the hills, the stately pines, the castle to the left. Deep on his mind was the question of why God kept stripping him of strength, not only from his brush with death, but more recently Evelyne's.

"Lord," he prayed aloud, "I know that You humble in order to exalt and weaken the body to strengthen the spirit. Further, I know that we cannot experience Your full power until ours is gone. I ask You to enable me to persevere in this process as You unfold the way You choose to glorify Yourself in my life. This is not easy. Often it's frightening. I want to faithfully follow, however, wherever You lead."

He leaned back to enjoy the fresh breeze, knowing that the future would not be presented on this day, but would unfold day by day as he walked in faith. He was full of anticipation to see how God would display His power. There was no way to know, however, that God intended to veer his path beyond Japan to the entire world.

CHAPTER TWENTY-NINE

Pathway to the World

Their furlough was to end on September 23, 1967, but by mid-August Ernst and Sigrid were fully packed for their third term in Japan. Ernst excitedly waved the shipping slip before Sigrid's eyes and said, "Well, we're just about under way. Soon we will be on the boat and heading back to our home in Japan."

"Ernst, you've come a long way from the village life of Goenningen," Sigrid said as she cleared the supper dishes from the table.

"God has certainly led us on a path I would never have designed," Ernst mused.

"Yes, indeed," Sigrid responded. "I hope He keeps us away from death's door for a long time."

"So do I. You know, Evelyne's brush with death impacted me far more deeply than my own. It's a lot easier to be the one dying than to watch your daughter dying."

"Yes, that was terrible, but thank God He gave her back to us."

"But here we are in the happiest days of our lives, Sigrid, returning together to the land and people we love."

The next day Ernst received a letter from Rev. Pflaum, the new mission director. Ernst expected some last-minute encouragement for his return to Japan. But he was wrong.

Opening the letter, Ernst read, "As you know, Rev. Hertel died three years ago. Pastor Walter took his place as overseas director, but he is elderly now and wants to phase out. We need a man to direct our foreign fields and to open new ones. I want you to consider staying here in Germany to take over that position."

Sweat beads formed across Ernst's thirty-eight-year-old brow, although he felt chilled in his spirit. His thoughts raced, *Sigrid and I have spent twelve years immersing ourselves in the Japanese culture. Surely our best days are still ahead. We have come to love these people as our own. Must we give that up now?*

Feeling as though a death sentence had just been pronounced, Ernst shared the letter with Sigrid. A sober atmosphere hung over the dinner table that night as they discussed the options before them.

"This is a most difficult decision, Sigrid. We both have such a love for the Japanese people that it will be hard not to return. We were prepared in Japan, but perhaps not necessarily for Japan alone. If this is from the Lord, we must obey. As much as we both love Japan, I feel that God is leading us in this other way. Unfortunately, this new position would require me to travel quite extensively."

"God gave me peace, Ernst, through the long days and nights you were away from home in Japan. Only once did I experience fear and loneliness during our two terms. It was a time when you were gone and I didn't yet know the people or speak the language well. I remember starting to cry as you left, but I turned away so that you would not see it. After that, the Lord gave me real peace.

"Your being away would not be the problem. Being near the familiar surroundings of Germany and the mission people is small consolation for my true concern. Besides taking care of the children, what will I do here? In Japan I shared a role in your ministry . . . but will I here too? And one more thing—your health held up in Japan, but will it hold up to traveling around the world?"

"I am sure, Sigrid, that the Lord will open a ministry for you here. And if we could trust God to keep me alive in Japan, surely we can trust Him to do so anywhere in the world."

"I will do what you think is right, but this is a very sudden change for me to face."

Ernst drew the discussion to a close by saying, "It's not what I was looking for, but I think we should do it. Sigrid, dear, we must think and pray about this matter."

The next day, Ernst took a long walk deep into the Black Forest. His prayer was like a conversation with God deep within his heart:

> *Father, I can almost hear the voice of Sister Lina Stahl crying out to You to make the mountain at Liebenzell like a volcano spewing out flames of the gospel around the world. And You certainly answered her prayer by establishing the mission on that very mountain. I am so thankful that I have been able to take a flame from the mountain to Japan, but this new job is too vast. Why would You call me to it?*

Scenes from his life unfolded as he walked the path of memory. Then Sigrid's face appeared before his mind. *You certainly gave me the right wife, Father. She is so trustworthy and committed to You and to me, but now she is suffering over this issue.*

He had to sit down while remembering his passage through the dark valley of death. A shaft of sunlight slanted through the pines, setting a small patch of forest floor mystically aglow. *Father, that's like the thin ray of light in that dismal hospital room by which I saw Your promises at the foot of my bed. Indeed, You proved Your love and power by sustaining my life. You arranged for the young doctor to return home from vacation just in time to help. You alone have kept me alive to this day. Only You could have given Sigrid and me more children, even delivering one from death. You showed me how self-determined and self-motivated I was in doing Your work. I am thankful and humbled by all of this. I can see the changes that have come into my heart. But now this new ministry . . . all new, and with so many different tasks.*

It was then that an answer arched like a flare across his mind: *I am a consuming fire. I have tested and refined both the mission and you. No one can adequately carry the fire of truth from the mountain without first being refined by fire. This isn't the time to question, but rather to obey. I have shaped you by My hand to take flames from the mountain to many corners of the world.*

At breakfast the next morning Ernst broke his intense silence. Sigrid was pouring coffee when he said with firm resolve, "I believe it is God's will for me to take this position. I'll tell Pastor Pflaum that we agree to do it." He tore the shipping slip into small pieces.

Sigrid took a deep breath and said, "It isn't easy for me, but I will support your decision, trusting it to be God's will."

The next day Ernst informed Rev. Pflaum of their decision. The position began with a transition period as Pastor Walter wound down his labor, giving Ernst time to learn the job and set forth plans for the future. He began to pray daily that the Lord would enable him for his new tasks.

Soon after he began, it became clear that both he and the mission were enlarging their vision at the same time. Ernst discovered this while doing the very thing he detested the most: attending "stuffy" meetings. It reminded him of the meetings he attended in his youth, while longing to play soccer instead. Every cell of his body screamed to be out doing something, not just talking. But he settled his nerves with the realization that he needed a clear understanding of the mission's history before he could advance its future.

It was a breezy spring morning. The windows of the third floor conference room were open. Chirping birds demanded attention. Ernst shifted often on the wooden chair that felt fossilized beneath him. The director started his briefing:

"As we all know, Liebenzell was founded by Rev. Heinrich Coerper when James Hudson Taylor asked him to begin a German branch of the China Inland Mission." Ernst's cheeks quivered as he swallowed a yawn. "On November 13, 1899, Coerper started the work which was known as The German Subsidiary of the China Inland Mission."

I gave up Japan for this? Ernst thought. *Hang in there. It must get better.*

"The name was changed to Liebenzell Mission—known as LM—when the work was moved to Bad Liebenzell." Ernst tapped the eraser end of a pencil on the table.

"Seven weeks later, in the first week of January 1900, Heinrich Witt went as the first missionary to China. LM grew so rapidly over the next six years that it had to administer its own personnel and develop its own place of service. Hunan Province in Central China became that place. Changsha was the city where we were headquartered, as well as where we had a hospital. In 1893, in a village near the city, a little boy named Mao Tse Tung was born."

Suddenly, Ernst was shaken out of his listlessness. He leaned forward and asked, "The leader of the Cultural Revolution?"

"Yes. Fifty-six years later he led the upheaval that expelled Christian missions from China."

"There were a number of Christian martyrs in that period," Ernst interjected.

"Indeed, those were horrific years. China remains closed to this day. This forced our mission into a time of transition, a new vision. We no longer have a mono-vision fixed on China."

Ernst pieced the rest of the puzzle together. "So that's what led to opening the works in Papua New Guinea, Micronesia, Japan and Taiwan."

"Yes, and that's the picture you inherit. You will be in charge of caring for all of those fields."

"But I'm committed to opening new fields as well."

"Yes, I understand that. In fact, that's the mission's agenda too. We have already agreed to that. But you will also have the care of the existing fields under your responsibility. Let's also discuss why we started works in the United States and Canada. Following World War II, countries would not take missionaries with a German visa. The Lord provided a marvelous resort center at Schooleys Mountain in New Jersey where the missionaries could stay while getting U.S. visas to various fields."

"So it sounds as if both the mission and I are undergoing an expansion of vision."

"Yes, that's true. By the way, how are you working through the change so far?"

"I had a long session with the Lord in the Black Forest—and I'll tell you that more than the forest was dark. My heart was very confused. I was convinced I was to return to Japan. But the Lord brought many testimonies of His past faithfulness to my mind. Finally, I realized that spiritual maturity is measured by one's willingness to be broken, even of cherished dreams. Clinging to Japan would have been my self-will insisting on what I loved. Counting on His future faithfulness, I am now ready to do my best in my new role."

CHAPTER THIRTY

Vision in Action

Years passed. The calendar read 1974. Ernst rose one morning at the first blush of day. Having showered to shock himself fully awake, he turned on a small desk lamp and opened his Bible. His lips moved silently, "Heavenly Father, I know that without faith it is impossible to please You. My heart's cry today is for faith to believe You for the impossible, to see You open doors around the world for the advance of the gospel. I don't want to repeat Israel's unbelievers who, having seen great miracles during the exodus from Egypt, failed to trust You for their daily supply in the desert. As I cross the hot deserts that lie ahead, help me to display faithful obedience."

Thus, with pragmatic faith, Ernst continued his daily routine of surveying needs in various countries, arranging for missionaries to go to the fields, negotiating with governments and indigenous church bodies, reporting to the mission board, traveling to open new fields while overseeing existing ones and much more.

"I have found the past years most helpful," Ernst said one day at a directors' meeting. "It has been hard to transition from missionary to overseas director. But the time has come now to act. Although our policy has been to wait on an invitation from a country, I believe the Lord would have us take the initiative ourselves."

"That's what we agreed to when you started. So, where would you like to start?" asked one director.

"Bangladesh. The civil war in that country has left many dead and wounded. There is great suffering, hunger and chaos. The country is in shambles. They need help. I believe it is the place to start."

There was a long, contemplative pause. This proposal carried incredible implications: It had never been done, people would face risk and the possibility of failure loomed before them. Finally, the silence was broken when one director said, "Yes, let's try!" All agreed.

After some days of strategy planning and much prayer by many at the mission, Ernst telephoned Pastor Goto in Japan. "Would you be able to meet me at the Calcutta Airport in two days? I need you to go to Bangladesh with me to give help and advice." Pastor Goto agreed enthusiastically, and the two discussed further plans.

By the time Ernst left the office that evening, he could feel a familiar weakness returning and spreading throughout his body. After dinner he confided to Sigrid that he was not sure he could make the trip. "We know how Satan fights," she insisted. "Ignore the weakness and get ready." He did, and his strength returned shortly before departure.

Pastor Goto, on the other hand, prepared with anticipation, knowing that life with Ernst was never dull. They met in Calcutta at the appointed time, but no one was sure if the airplane for Bangladesh would arrive. The lounge filled with people. Time dragged. Then came the unexpected. Pastor Goto said, "Look at that lady entering the lounge. She looks like a missionary."

"Yes," Ernst replied, "and look at that man over there. Look at his shoes, belt and tie. He looks like another German going to Bangladesh. Why don't you talk to the woman and find out who she is, and I'll go to the man. Let's meet back here in ten minutes." Soon they reunited with their stories.

Mr. Goto started, "She's a Lutheran missionary from Finland and is going to northern Bangladesh."

"That's good," Ernst said, "maybe she can help us when we get there. The man I talked to comes from Bavaria and is a representative for Siemens Medical Instruments. He's on his way to see the Health Minister of Bangladesh, who has asked him for an X-ray machine. His only problem is that they have no X-ray technician."

Goto's eyes brightened. "You have technicians among the Liebenzell sisters who could fill that role."

"Precisely. But it doesn't stop there. He's going to stay in the same hotel as us. He said that he'll try to arrange a meeting for us with the Health Minister."

Finally, the plane did arrive, and as the two men flew to Bangladesh, they had a deep sense of praise for what appeared to be God leading their footsteps even before departure. The next day, Ernst and Pastor Goto sought other contacts throughout the capital city. Not only were there no opportunities for ministry, neither did they see the Siemens representative. The following day was the same.

Thursday night, Ernst and Rev. Goto read the Scriptures and prayed together. "If nothing happens tomorrow, we'll return home," Ernst said. "We must not force anything. This may be a sign that the Lord is not leading us in this direction."

Just as Ernst was entering a deep sleep, the phone rang. Groggily he fumbled to get the receiver to his ear, and sputtered out a hello.

"Mr. Vatter. This is the representative of Siemens Medical Instruments. You have an appointment with the Health Minister at 10:30 tomorrow morning." Ernst thanked him and enjoyed a good night's rest.

At 10:30 sharp the next morning Ernst and Mr. Goto began to negotiate with the Minister of Health.

"Can you provide two Liebenzell sisters to do X-ray work?" asked the Minister.

"Yes, but in light of the situation here, I am concerned that it is too dangerous to send only two women."

"Well, send a dozen. That will be fine."

"Wouldn't it be better to send at least one couple with them?"

Amazed at Ernst's persistence the minister replied, "Yes, yes, that will be fine. Send couples too."

Knowing that political people can make promises that never get fulfilled, Ernst doggedly pressed further: "Excuse me, but I must make one more important request."

"What's that?" responded the Minister, who by that point was feeling as worn down as Pharaoh against Moses.

"Excellency, would you be so kind as to ask your secretary to write down what you have just told me so that I have something in hand to present to my board?" Ernst was also concerned that he would need written proof for other officials in Bangladesh to see as well.

"Gladly. My secretary will type it while we are at lunch."

The next day at the airport, Ernst and Pastor Goto sat together to wait for their flights. "It was wonderful to be with you, Ernst, and to watch how the Lord opened the door to this country."

"Yes, I'm full of joy today. This is the first time Liebenzell Mission has entered a country without first receiving an invitation. We're committed, however, to cooperate and not compete with existing mission groups, since it would be foolish and dishonorable to the Lord to duplicate efforts. I sense that this is a new era for us. Look at how the Lord led us to our main contact for Bangladesh before leaving the airport in Calcutta. The Lord is going to open many new doors."

Pastor Goto departed for Japan and Ernst for Germany. The very next day, Ernst was in his office arranging for one couple, Albert and Marianne Rechkemmer, and two women, Sisters Gertrud Endlich and Charlotte Andres—a nurse and an X-ray technician—to go to Bangladesh. Weeks later, on April 26, 1974, Ernst was on the airplane accompanying them to the field. As they traveled, one missionary asked where they would stay.

"Stay?" responded Ernst. "Oh, in a tent," he replied, always ready for a joke. "The war has destroyed so much that a tent is all we have. That's why I'm going with you. I'll work on finding lodging but, if necessary, we'll start in a tent—together. Let's pray, since a permanent place to live and operate will be nearly impossible to find."

Fortunately, despite Ernst's jesting, they were able to stay in a hotel, where they would gather in their free moments with other foreigners around the swimming pool. One day someone told Ernst about a two-story house that a general had for rent. Ernst called him immediately, and they met two days later. The general was a medium-built man with a round friendly face, brown skin and black hair.

He was soft spoken, but had a strong, confident personality. Further, he was a man of his word.

"Well, Mr. Vatter," said the general as he poked his glasses further back on his nose, "the representative from the world bank also wants to rent the house."

"We certainly cannot compete with what he could pay, but I can assure you that your home will be immaculately kept if you rent it to us."

"Come back in two days for my answer."

For two days the five prayed that the Lord would direct the general's heart. Then Ernst returned.

"Mr. Vatter," said the general, folding his arms across his blue shirt, "having my home and garden kept in good condition is more important than having more money. The house is yours."

"I will not see you again, since I will be returning to Germany. But I want to thank you and reassure you that your house and garden will be well cared for."

They shook hands. Now the missionaries had both a home and a place from which to work. Liebenzell's latest effort was underway.

But Ernst had little opportunity to savor the victory, as the many details of his daily routine occupied his time. Weeks turned into months, and months became years; however, they were not always filled with the mundane. Through the prayers and labor of many, Ernst saw the work of the mission extend from the mainland of Papua New Guinea to nearby New Britain. Then the doors opened to Africa—first in Liberia and next in Zambia.

Success continued to unfold for one simple reason: Ernst did not believe God because he saw miracles; rather, he saw miracles because he believed in God. His faith was practical, though. Often he acted long before the means to accomplish a task became visible.

Sometimes, however, God's wisdom was beyond understanding and Ernst longed for a miracle, but saw none.

CHAPTER THIRTY-ONE

Wisdom Beyond Understanding

March 27, 1977. Deep in the evening in southern Bangladesh sat Johannes Werner, who had said good-bye to his wife and family in Germany in order to spend six months building a medical clinic for the Liebenzell Mission. He had enjoyed a refreshing bath and was sitting alone in the partially built structure, thinking about home.

"Mr. Werner?" questioned a harsh voice out of the dark.

Surprised, he spun toward the voice and found himself staring into the barrel of a gun.

"We know you have money to pay the people working for you. Where is it? Get it! Now!"

"Yes, the money is here. But I need it to build this clinic to help *your* people."

"Get it now!" the man snarled.

Johannes' fingers trembled as he took the bag of money from a tool kit. The thought of being shot seemed surreal. He lifted the bag and turned to hand it to the robbers, saying, "I want you to know that Jesus . . ."

There was a sudden white flash, an ear splitting *crack!* and the man's labor of love became the sacrifice of his life. Johannes saw and felt nothing as his body flew backward and dropped lifelessly to the floor. At home an unknowing wife prayed for her husband's safe return home. The prayer was answered. He went safely home . . . his heavenly home.

* * *

Back in Germany, Ernst was returning from a successful trip overseas with Pastor Pflaum. But any celebration over their accomplishments was short-lived. They were greeted at the airport with the shocking news that Johannes Werner had been murdered just two nights before. Ernst felt as though he himself had just been shot in the chest.

Immediately, the two men drove to Leonbrunn to express their deep sympathy for the Werner family's loss. They found Johannes' grieving wife Christel at home with her five children: Christine, Renate, Annedore, Markus and Susanne.

After praying with the family, Ernst struggled to ask a difficult question: "Mrs. Werner, I need to know what you want to have done with the body of your dear husband."

"Please have him returned home, so that at least we'll have a grave to visit."

Heavy in heart, Ernst and Pastor Pflaum stood to leave. They had committed the Werner family to the Lord and were touched by young Christine's reassuring words: "Mommy, it's really good that Daddy loved the Lord Jesus, isn't it?"

"Yes, dear, yes." Christel brushed her hand through her daughter's hair while Christine gently leaned her head against her mother's shoulder. Two people needing comfort sought to comfort each other.

Fortunately, the Liebenzell Mission had a good insurance policy on Mr. Werner, which would greatly assist Christel and her family in their loss. However, Christel's friends and the Liebenzell Mission family didn't let it stop there. They joined together to build her a two-story home, a beautiful expression of love to assist her into the future.

* * *

Not everyone had the Werner family's spiritual maturity for handling bad news. Some years later when Ernst was visiting the Liebenzell Mission in Zambia, he chatted with Sister Gunhilde Rott. She had mastered the Zambian language and endeared herself to the people by attending numerous women's meetings. A contagiously friendly personality helped win her a place in the Zambian hearts.

"Did you know, Ernst, that the ladies have honored Gunhilde with a uniform from the Women's Association?" asked one missionary. Gunhilde dipped her face into her hand and blushed.

"Really? What is it like?"

"Oh, it's a beautiful blue skirt with a red blouse and white scarf. It's their way of honoring her."

"Sister Gunhilde," said Ernst, "please put it on so that I can take a picture of you in it. I want to show everyone in Germany, especially your father. I know he's not a believer and this might impress him."

Gunhilde dipped her face deeper behind her hand, leaving only her eyebrows showing, and said, "Sorry, Mr. Vatter, but I don't have it with me. Maybe another time."

"All right, but be sure to bring that outfit with you on your furlough next year because I want to see you in it. We are all pleased and proud of your success."

"Thank you. Yes, I will bring it, but understand that it's my privilege to be serving the Lord here."

Ernst returned to Germany. Months rolled by before the fateful Sunday when a phone call from Zambia brought tragic news. Amid the drop-outs and delays on the phone line, the mission staff was informed that Sister Gunhilde had been shot and killed by three bandits who stole her car.

Several days later Ernse went to the home of her seventy-year-old father. Mr. Rott's son had taken over his bakery shop, but all his hopes were in his daughter's return from Zambia to care for him. Ernst knocked on the door and was greeted by Mr. Rott, who was still reeling with shock.

"Mr. Rott, I'm Ernst Vatter with the Liebenzell Mission. On behalf of the mission I have come to express our deepest sympathy and to let you know that are praying for your family. I hope it is of comfort to you to know that your daughter lived and died doing what she loved most—serving the Lord."

There was a pause as Mr. Rott stared at Ernst in disbelief. Then, burying his head in his hands, he rocked back and forth sobbing and asking the unanswerable question: "Can you tell me why God took my daughter? My daughter was only in her thirties. Why did God do this? How could He do this?"

Ernst answered, "Often the wisdom of God cannot be understood in this lifetime. That doesn't take away the pain of loss for any of us. But it is the faith we cling to—confidence that God is all knowing. We cannot understand his ways, we can only trust Him." But Gunhilde's grief-stricken father could not accept his words.

Hundreds of people gathered for Gunhilde's funeral. They gathered from both her natural family and her Liebenzell family. Ernst entered the chapel and walked to the casket. There she lay wearing the blue skirt, red blouse and white scarf . . . in final rest.

CHAPTER THIRTY-TWO

Blinded by Long Hair

The Liebenzell Mission was rapidly expanding, but not without suffering. Ernst had no choice but to force himself beyond the painful losses of Johannes and Gunhilde. Absorbed in work, he barely noticed the days and years speeding by like one-way road signs. The streaks of gray appearing amid his shock of dark brown hair seemed strange to him. He became a regular sight passing through the Stuttgart Airport. Ticket agents would smile and ask, "Where in the world are you going now, Mr. Vatter?" And that's literally what he was doing—darting around the globe.

He was pounded by two pressures that preceded nearly every trip: One was the continued plaguing of his body with physical pain and weakness; the other was strange family disturbances, unusual arguments and conflicts. Both he and Sigrid felt sure that these were satanic assaults designed to stop him from advancing the Liebenzell Mission's outreach.

However, there was one area of concern that haunted Ernst, and that was the spiritual well-being of his family. One morning, as he was preparing for a trip to Micronesia, he arose for his regular meeting with God. On this particular morning he was struck anew by Jesus' words, "If anyone comes to me and does not hate his father and mother, his wife and children, his brothers and sisters—yes, even his own life—he cannot be my disciple" (Luke 14:26). There was a deep tearing in his heart. He sensed a threat warning him not to go, otherwise he'd lose his family. His physical symptoms intensified. Knowing the difference between the Holy Spirit's quiet, peaceful way and Satan's threat-filled attacks, Ernst said out loud, "Father, into Your hands I commend my family."

Shafts of morning sunlight illuminated his little desk. Looking up, he prayed, *Lord, it's not easy to follow You, but it is all I can do. I must obey You, but my heart is troubled. Dare I seek to save the world at the risk of losing my own family? My own dear son hardly knows me, but far worse, he doesn't know You. I pray for his salvation. I hear the laughter of my three little girls maturing each time I return from a trip. I feel as though I am the loser for not being able to trace their growth day by day. Still, I will hold nothing back as I serve You, knowing that You withhold no good thing from me. I trust Your faithful care for my family.*

Before noon his jet lifted from the runway with a deafening roar and nosed toward Japan. From there his flight would continue to Guam and then Micronesia. Thoughts about his family lingered heavily throughout the trip.

Reaching the Micronesian Islands, located in the far west Pacific just north of the equator, Ernst was scheduled to visit missionaries on Guam, Palau and Truk. Five days after his arrival a telegram arrived from Sigrid. It read, "Dear Ernst, Norman was converted at the summer camp."

"Ah, I cannot contain my joy," he said at the meeting where plans were being made to expand the mission work. "My son has just become a believer!" Everyone shared in his happiness.

That night as he prayed, Ernst was filled with thanks, but his heart remained heavy. The same deep feeling of threat returned and persisted until his trip home two weeks later.

Ernst longed to be with his family, but would first have to endure the long flights to Tokyo and then on to Germany. Nostalgia quickened when he found himself surrounded by several newly married Japanese couples returning to Tokyo. The couple beside him spoke freely, not knowing that he understood what they were saying.

"I will carry you in my arms. You are my little bird, the flower of my heart," swooned the young husband. His bride smiled and made a cooing sound in response. Each word inflamed seemingly unquenchable emotions in the young couple. The plane was alive with joy.

Ernst smiled mischievously and thought, *My, if he carries her in his arms as he said, he'll soon have a bad back.* He chuckled, thinking of the day when his own children would be in the fatal grasp of such bliss.

Eventually his mind geared toward work. As the jumbo jet sliced through the silvery blue sky, he pulled a notepad from his briefcase to jot some notes about his many meetings over the past weeks. Suddenly, screams came from the first-class section. Ernst looked up to see smoke rolling along the ceiling toward him. Flight attendants scurried to the cockpit, then returned and started ripping out the ceiling panels, frantically searching for the source of the fire. Thick grayish smoke billowed. People gagged and coughed. The loud screaming only exacerbated the blind confusion.

"We're going to die!" a panicked passenger screamed.

"Do something, fast!" implored another.

The highly trained pilot spoke over the intercom in a calming voice. "Do not be afraid. We will get the situation under control. Please be quiet. We are doing all we can."

Realizing that their dreams may never reach day's end, the newlyweds around Ernst wept openly. Ernst looked out the window and prayed, *Lord, I would like to go home and see my wife and children again. Was this morning our last time together? Does it all end today?*

He continued praying, not out of panic, but from the depth of his heart. The anger and pride that once walled his heart had over the years been replaced by the shield of faith. This day, however, something special and new occurred. An unannounced thought swept through his entire being, stronger than an audible voice: "I am the Good Shepherd. I know my sheep." The thought was accompanied by a profound assurance that he would be safe. This peace dispelled the threat and held him firmly as the wheels of the jet touched the runway and slowed to a safe stop in Japan. Fire trucks and ambulances surrounded the plane as the relieved passengers slid down emergency chutes to safety.

For the remainder of the trip, Ernst replayed in his mind the unique phenomenon of having God enfold him in unsurpassed peace. He thought, *God, if You can speak such assurance directly to my heart, surely I can trust You with my family.* He wrote on a piece of paper: *This experience is the exception, not the rule. Now I must trust God's Word with my will and not rely on experiences. God gives such special moments at His own discretion. Now I must trust God's Word with my will and not rely on experience.* Ernst would soon have the opportunity to put that statement to the test.

He returned to his home that perched high on a hill over-looking the small town of Calw, situated in the Black Forest just ten miles south of Bad Liebenzell. Excitement stirred as the family gathered for dinner. Dad was home. As usual, Ernst sat at the head of the large table and Sigrid sat to his right. Norman, who was now sixteen, sat at his dad's left. Iris, who was nearing her fifteenth birthday, sat beside Sigrid. To Norman's left sat eleven-year-old Anette, and Evelyne who was eight.

It should have been a time of celebrating, but Ernst had lost the joy with which he entered the house. Instead he sat sullen and silent. After dinner, Sigrid met him in the sloping backyard. "What's wrong, Ernst?"

"I thought you said Norman was converted."

"He is."

"Then how can he still be wearing that long hair? It's all the way down to his shoulders."

"What are you saying, Ernst? That a person cannot be a Christian with long hair?"

"No, it's not that . . . but one would think that if he's converted in his heart, then his head would show it. Why doesn't he cut his hair?"

"Ernst, you are only concerned about your reputation in light of the legalistic thinking of some other Christians. It's nonsense to think that conversion means automatic con-formity to a certain appearance. It's not so. I believe he is as converted as you or me."

Ernst loosened his necktie and cleared his throat in an ef-fort to ease his mental pressure. For weeks he told no one lo-cally about his son's alleged conversion, uncertain that it was genuine.

Later that summer Ernst was driving his little Volkswagen Beetle through the Black Forest on a bright Sunday afternoon. Swerving to miss a squirrel, he became hopelessly stuck in a ditch. Many well-dressed people—some perhaps Christians—drove past, ignoring his plight. Ernst leaned against his car, looked toward the sky and prayed, "Lord, will You send help to me?"

Fortunately the day was pleasant, and Ernst listened to the birds chatter as he bathed his face in the sunlight. Eventually he heard a car in the distance, but assumed it would pass by like all the rest. He was surprised, however, when the small car rounded the corner and slowed to a stop. Out jumped four young people in skin-tight clothing. Ernst's eyes widened as their three-inch-high spiked hair glistened in the sun in brilliant greens and yellows.

"Got a problem, Grandpop?" asked the driver.

Shaking off his shock, Ernst replied, "Yes, I'm stuck."

"No problem, Pop."

The four leaned hard against the car as Ernst tramped on the gas. Back up on the road popped "Pop."

"How much do I owe you?" asked Ernst.

The driver slowly looked at Ernst from head to toe, then said, "Nothing. You need your money yourself. Cheerio, Pop." And they were off.

The lesson was clear. One cannot judge people by their appearance. The well-dressed people left him in the ditch, while young people who looked alien to planet Earth showed kindness.

Slowly a distant memory began to emerge from Ernst's past. He pictured his mentor Willie bent over with laughter as he said, *Many Christians have silly ideas that you must ignore.* That had been his response when Ernst told him about the man who accused him of not being born again because he had *curly* hair. Whap! Ernst's face flushed with shame as he realized he had been blinded by his own foolish legalism.

Neither should Norman be judged by his appearance, only by his heart, admitted Ernst to himself. The veteran missionary-saint submitted to a deeper lesson.

Any lingering doubts about the genuineness of Norman's conversion were erased when one night, later that year, Ernst was awakened from a sound sleep. "Daddy . . . Daddy," a gentle voice whispered. It was Norman.

"Yes, what is it? What's wrong?"

"Daddy, I couldn't sleep. I lied to you today and must confess it. I can't sleep knowing that I lied to you."

"It's all right, son, it's all right. Thank you for waking me. All is forgiven."

Norman slipped back to his bedroom as Ernst felt the pillow becoming damp beneath his cheek. Through this event he saw into his son's heart. *Lord, forgive me for doubting You*, he prayed. *I asked You to save my son. You did it, yet I doubted it because of his long hair. Thank You for fulfilling Your promise to me.*

Norman's quiet temperament, much like Sigrid's, was often hard to read. Thus it was years later, after he had married a fine young woman named Conny and they had five children, that Ernst gained still more insight into his son's spiritual depth.

"Daddy, I've called for a terrible reason. Conny went upstairs to tend to Rouven. He . . ." Norman's voice broke. "He . . . he was cold. Our little baby is dead."

Sigrid, who was listening, exhaled a deep groan. Ernst stood paralyzed in silence.

"Daddy, will you speak at Rouven's burial?"

"Yes, yes, Norman, of course. Please tell Conny that we are fully behind both of you."

"Daddy, the pain of this has done something to me. I knew how to pray before, but now I know how to cry out to the Lord."

"I understand, Norman."

Ernst walked to the backyard and wept, not only for the loss of his youngest grandchild, but for the increasing evidence of Norman's heartfelt conversion to Jesus Christ. He looked toward the setting sun and prayed aloud, "Lord, I am guilty of judging people on my own terms, not Yours. Forgive me. Change me. Help me to look past appearance to see the heart. Let not my judgmental spirit damage Your craftsmanship in others. Help me to love people who are different than I—even my enemies."

The test of that prayer was soon at hand. Could Ernst love the French, remembering the inhuman abuse of the prison camp?

CHAPTER THIRTY-THREE

Back to the Rhine Bridge

The years scrolled forward to 1985. One day, while reading various mission reports, Ernst realized there were more born-again Christians in Cameroon than in the Roman Catholic-based countries of Italy, Spain, Portugal, France and Belgium—combined. Leaning back in his chair, he put his pencil to his lips and pondered: *France is just across the Rhine. We have been going to the ends of the world while our neighbors remain lost. Why shouldn't we go to France? The French are people whom God loves too.*

Suddenly it struck him. He was concerned for the spiritual well-being of people whom he once bitterly hated. Pastor Bitterhof's words replayed across the screen of memory: *God tests the depth of our spiritual growth by seeing if we will love and serve the thing we hate. I suspect that someday you will be tested to see if you will serve the French.* Ernst wondered at which point in the seventy-times-seven process of forgiveness the fire of bitterness had been overcome in his heart. He couldn't remember. All he knew was that as Joseph served the Egyptians and Daniel served the Babylonians, so he was now free to serve the French. From that day onward he began praying for a sign about opening a work in France.

He made known his desire to start a work in France in the Liebenzell publication, considering it a fleece: If the idea to bring the gospel to France was not of God, then there would be no interest. If it was of God, then interest would emerge. He prayed daily for clear direction.

"Good morning," Ernst cheerily greeted as he entered his office at the mission headquarters one morning.

"Good morning," responded his secretary. "There's a letter on your desk from a doctor's wife in France that I think will be of interest to you. Her name is Mrs. Wenger."

Ernst picked up the letter and walked to a window overlooking a slope with pines jutting to the sky like nature's steeples. He was surprised to see that the letter was written in German.

> *Dear Mr. Vatter, The ministry of the Liebenzell Mission is of great interest to me. The founder and I were good friends. I read that you are interested in starting a work in France. That makes me very happy indeed. I want to strongly encourage you to do so. My husband has passed away, and I have more time to think about such matters. Please keep me informed of your intentions.*

Ernst stepped into the outer office and said to his secretary, "This is an interesting letter."

"Yes, I agree. Do you think this is God's answer to your prayers? Is it time to advance into France?"

"There's no way that this one letter is a clear indication of that; after all, it will take a lot more than one kind letter to start a work. We'll have to continue praying about France."

With that, Ernst entered his office to prepare messages for a missionary conference. After a long afternoon of writing sermon outlines, he walked to the window and took a deep breath of satisfaction. The pines on top of the hills were bathed in the light of the evening sun. *Thank You, Lord*, he prayed, *for the amazing team of people that You have brought to the Liebenzell Mission and the opportunities before us.* Before returning home for dinner, he squeezed one more item into his day. He lifted the phone and dialed Gerd Grosshans, the business manager of the mission.

"Hello, this is Ernst. I would like you to drive to Switzerland with me tomorrow. I need to tend to some business and thought we could visit a Mrs. Wenger on the way home. She's a doctor's wife who wrote to me, saying she is excited that we want to open a work in France."

"Oh, that's wonderful. Certainly, I'll accompany you."

"Very good. We'll leave at 7 a.m."

By 9 the next morning they were within ten minutes of Strasbourg, the town where Mrs. Wenger lived in a retirement home. They stopped at a public phone.

"Hello, Mrs. Wenger, this is Ernst Vatter. You wrote to me at the Liebenzell Mission."

"Oh, yes. I hope you still plan to begin a work here in France."

"That is our desire. I want to speak with you about that. My business manager and I will be returning from other business in Switzerland about 2 o'clock this afternoon. Could we come to see you?"

"No, I'd rather not meet you here. I'll meet you at the Rhine Bridge at 2 o'clock. I'll be alone in a small French-made car."

"All right, we'll see you then."

The strong sun had raised the temperature beyond eighty by the time they arrived at the bridge that afternoon.

"There, that must be her," said Mr. Grosshans as they pulled up alongside a car near the bridge.

"Hello, are you Mrs. Wenger?"

"Yes, are you Mr. Vatter?"

"I am. Can we take you to a little cafeteria for some coffee while we talk?"

"No," was the reply from the small, medium-weight woman who looked to be in her eighties. "Don't waste the mission's money. Just get in and we'll talk here." Her voice was high-pitched, but exuded confidence. She was energetic and, with lively animation, asked a steady flow of questions about Liebenzell before narrowing the discussion to France. The mid-afternoon sun beat down upon the little car. It was scorching hot, and there was no breeze to rescue Ernst from the heat. Far below, the cool waters of the Rhine rushed by.

"Did you have any specific thoughts or questions about France?" Ernst asked as the visit was stretching toward an hour.

"Yes, most certainly. What are your plans for France?"

"We do not have any funds to start, but are researching what other missions are doing so that we do not duplicate efforts. Also, we want to determine where the most needy place is to begin."

"Normandy," she commanded. "That's where to start— Normandy. Not only was that the landing site on D day, but it is the most lacking of the gospel. Buy a castle and start a work at Normandy."

"A castle?" Ernst responded incredulously while fumbling to regain composure.

"Yes, a castle. There are many for sale right now, and I think the Lord's work should be done in a castle."

"It's about time for us to leave," said Gerd, trying to save Ernst from the sudden awkwardness of the moment. They opened the doors and started to get out.

"Wait one moment," said Mrs. Wenger. "Here is a package for you, Mr. Vatter."

Ernst settled back into his seat and opened what looked like a shoe box. When he had unwound the string and removed the wrapping, he lifted the lid to see money—a whole stack of it!

"There's 30,000 German marks to help you get started," Mrs. Wenger said.

Astonished, Ernst blurted out, "But that isn't enough to buy a castle."

"What kind of a man are you? You are quite frank, aren't you? Can't you wait? Perhaps I can do more later."

"Please forgive me, I'm sorry. It's just that you had me thinking about castles . . . and . . . I'm very sorry. I don't mean any offense. Of course I am both surprised and full of gratitude."

After thanking Mrs. Wenger profusely, Ernst felt a special evening glow in his heart as he and Gerd returned to Liebenzell. He thought to himself, *It was not too many miles to the north that the American soldiers saved me from being carried by the French into a lost future. Only God could have orchestrated that. Now, today, I sit on a bridge crossing the same river and am handed 30,000 marks to take the gospel to France. God is full of grace and ingenuity.*

At his side, there was a concern looming in Mr. Grosshans' heart that held him in a choke hold of silence. Ernst knew what was wrong, so he decided to bring it to light. "I realize that I nearly blew it today with my abruptness," he admitted.

"Yes, I think you did. You hardly seemed grateful for such a sizeable gift."

"I know. First, the gift surprised me. But secondly, I've always found it hard to use many words to say thank you. I know people need that and wish that I could be that way. But I feel insincere saying thank you too much. I think it goes back to my problem of viewing uprightness and straightforwardness as the same. That got me into trouble in Japan. I hope it won't do the same in France."

Twice over the next two years, Mrs. Wenger invited Ernst to return to see her. Each time she was able to release more money to the Liebenzell Mission, which helped tremendously in starting the work in France. Ernst never did buy a castle, knowing that the upkeep would be staggering and also that a woman who did not want to waste a few cents on coffee would not want to waste large sums of money on maintaining a castle, especially since it would not help to touch lives with the gospel.

Six years later, Ernst noted their progress in France: "Started in Normandy in 1987; forged into the cities of Coutances and Avranches in September 1988. Advanced into the city of St. Aubin in 1990, and penetrated the cities of Carentan and Alencon in September 1991."

Late one evening Ernst found himself in a reflective mood. He mused, *Look at the loss I would have suffered had I allowed my hatred for the French to rule over my heart. Thank You, Lord, for each test.*

Little did he know that one of the biggest tests of his faith was yet to spring upon him.

CHAPTER THIRTY-FOUR

Weathered Faith Tried Again

As the sun stealthily rose, giving dawn to a new day, Ernst sat at his little desk, Bible open. He felt complete that morning as he contemplated God's faithfulness with regard to his family. His oldest daughter Iris—at her father's suggestion—had decided to serve as a Liebenzell missionary in the African country of Burundi. The two youngest girls, Anette and Evelyne, both married, had made commitments to prepare as Liebenzell missionaries as well. And Norman had committed himself to support his sisters. Ernst could not have felt better when his finger landed on Psalm 62:5, "Find rest, O my soul, in God alone . . ."

Ernst made a note: *The word "rest" means silence, repose, completion. Just as God rested on the seventh day of creation, so He invites me to rest in Him.* He felt comfortably snuggled in his faith; after all, God had drawn their entire family to Christian salvation and service. However, he unwittingly failed to notice the ending of the quote, "Find rest, O my soul, *in God alone.*" His solitude would soon be shaken when he discovered what the previous hours had brought upon his oldest daughter.

* * *

Burundi, 2 o'clock in the morning: Iris shot straight up in bed. The black of night surrounded her as she again heard the percussive pounding sounds that had awakened her from a sound sleep. *They're shelling downtown!* she thought. *That's only a mile away.* Wondering what the capital city of Bujumbura would look like at dawn, she prayed for safety and fell back to sleep. She did not yet know that the tensions between the Tutsi and Hutu people had erupted again.

Iris had been stationed in Muramvya, a mountain range province about thirty-five miles from the capital. She was working with the Episcopal church on plans to develop a healthcare center. After weeks of establishing a strategy for the center, she had gone to the capital with a friend named Evi Stunz to spend a night in the home of missionaries Juergen and Monika Wiegel. Evi was ending a two-week visit and planned to catch a morning flight back to Germany.

Reawakened at 6:30 a.m., Iris walked through the house thinking and praying. All was silent, eerily still. As the team leader she had to put an action plan in motion. She met Juergen in the living room.

"Good morning, Juergen. I wonder how serious the problem is."

"I don't know. Let's turn on the news." There was nothing; no news at all. No one was talking about the fighting, which both missionaries knew was a sure sign of serious trouble.

* * *

In Germany Sigrid was arranging the breakfast table when she made the innocent comment, "I wonder how Iris is doing?"

"I don't know," Ernst replied, "but I had some wonderful thoughts while reading the Scriptures this morning. I know that Iris is serving in a special place. I'm so glad that she was open to working in Burundi."

* * *

Juergen's wife sleepily joined them in the room. Evi had entered as well. "I'm getting some news from Rwanda," Juergen said. The radio scratched and buzzed as he adjusted the dial. Soon they heard a faint voice saying: "There was heavy shelling through the night in Bujumbura, the capital of Burundi, as a *coup d'etat* was staged. The nation is paralyzed by widespread fighting."

The four looked at each other, fully realizing the disruption—even danger—of their lives.

"I wonder if this will affect my flight?" Evi pondered aloud. Following breakfast they departed for the airport.

"Halt! You cannot go beyond this point," barked a soldier.

"But, sir, we need to take our friend to the airport," Juergen explained.

"No flights today. Turn around and go back." The soldier's finger pointed back the way they had come as rigidly as his rifle.

"Let's go back to the house and think through our options," said Iris. They returned to the Wiegels' suburban home and brewed a fresh pot of coffee. The familiar odor offered a friendly comfort.

Iris drew silent as she thought, *Routine . . . we must reestablish a routine to help us gain a sense of direction.* Still, confusion confronted them. "I'm going to call Germany to let my parents and the Mission know we're all right," Iris announced as she lifted the receiver, then put it back down. "Dead. It's dead. There's no way to get through."

Sigrid and Ernst fell silent as they heard the British Broadcasting Company blaring: "There was a *coup d'etat* last night in Burundi. The capital was pounded by heavy artillery throughout the night. Damage and casualties are not known. Sporadic fighting is breaking out all over the country and everything is shut down. The United Nations is calling an emergency meeting to assess the problem."

Ernst grabbed the phone to call Iris in Burundi.

"Dead, Sigrid. Everything is dead." He soberly slipped into his little study, while Sigrid wiped her dry hands on her apron and walked to the back yard. Alone with their thoughts, they each lifted up their daughter before the Lord in prayer.

"I feel as though I'm in shock," said Monika. "We need to read the Scriptures and pray. Only the Lord can lead us now."

"Numb is how I feel," said Juergen. He opened his Bible to Psalm 46:6-7 and began to read: "Nations are in uproar, kingdoms fall; he lifts his voice, the earth melts. The LORD Almighty is with us; the God of Jacob is our fortress."

Bewilderment was replaced by assurance. God's sovereignty over events was clear, even over seemingly random and violent events. Juergen continued to read: "Come and see the works of the LORD, the desolations he has brought on the earth. He makes wars cease to the ends of the earth; he breaks the bow and shatters the spear, he burns the shields with fire. 'Be still, and know that I am God; I will be exalted among the nations, I will be exalted in the earth.'

The LORD Almighty is with us; the God of Jacob is our fortress" (46:8-11).

Suddenly, Iris felt a deep peace enfold her; the same divine peace that had enveloped her dad on the burning jet. She sensed God speaking clearly, though inaudibly, to her heart: *The safest place for you to be is in My will.*

"Why are you smiling, Iris?" asked Monika.

"Those verses are so reassuring. Two things are abundantly clear: First, the God who causes desolations also brings wars to an end. Everything conforms to His will and purpose. Second, I sense that God is saying to us that He will personally care for us amid this national turmoil. Certainly we face danger, but I have an unexplainable assurance of God's protection upon us. He has made promises that cannot be revoked."

* * *

A few days later Evi was finally able to depart from Burundi. For two weeks Iris stayed with the Wiegels. One day Iris said, "I would like to go back to my station to see if the Christians there survived."

"I'll go with you," said Juergen.

While the distance was only thirty-five miles, the road snaked 4,500 feet up an alpine-like road to Muramvya. Iris' heart raced and her breathing became rapid as they approached the scene. Then came a shower of relief as she saw the village intact and heard the people milling about. Though she longed to stay, the conditions upcountry were still unstable. Just traveling to the area had required taking a great step of faith, and she knew it was best to return to Bujumbura and stay with Juergen and Monika.

Later that night she was finally able to secure a phone connection with Germany and talk with her parents.

"Iris, it's so good to hear you! Tell us exactly what is happening. One U.S. magazine is showing pictures of thousands of dead bodies strewn along roadways. Is it really that bad there?"

"It's bad, Daddy. Many are without medical care, and there are tens of thousands of displaced people. They're frightened and starving."

"Do you want to come home?" Ernst questioned. "I'll arrange it immediately. It's so dangerous there."

"No, Daddy, I must stay. You taught me that the best place to be is always in the will of God. I have the assurance that I'm to stay and that He will be with me." Iris paused then added, "And Mom and Dad, please tell the Mission that it is my decision to stay here. If anything happens to me, they are not responsible."

Ernst felt chilled as he replied, "It will be done as you have requested. But your mother and I love you dearly, so please take care."

"I will."

* * *

Some weeks later, a missionary nurse, Regine Brenninger, joined Iris. They drew strength from each other as they passed through heavy days of human horror. Some days they mended broken bodies, while hearing the crackle of gunfire on the other side of the hospital wall. On other days, they walked through refugee camps feeding porridge to bewildered and desperate people.

"I feel sure, Regine, that we will always be safe in God's will, even if He calls us home in death. Our task is to trust in Him." With that, the two missionaries endured the turmoil.

* * *

Ernst had a harder time than anyone as he sought to entrust Iris to God. One day, as anxiety and peace wrestled against each other in his heart, he went to the top of "fire mountain" to think and pray. The tall pines always inspired hope as they pointed heavenward.

"Father," he began aloud, "You rarely give me rest from stretching my faith. I know that faith is the bridge that crosses from natural strength to Your strength. It's not always an easy bridge to cross, especially when I don't know the outcome: whether You will protect Iris or call her home as a martyr.

"It was one thing to cross that bridge as it related to my own life and ministry, but quite another to cross it as it relates to my daughter. Growing in faith doesn't get easier, since the stakes keep getting higher. But I also know that it is a sin not to trust You, and I do not wish to sin against You in this way. Forgive me for finding this crossing to be so difficult. I find myself trembling inside, but I stay resolved to trust You. While Iris is now out of my reach, she's not out of Your hands. I know that You will care for her in whatever way will most glorify You, and that I want above all else."

Then, one day God lightened Ernst's burden with an unusual surprise.

CHAPTER THIRTY-FIVE

A Voice From the Past

"**I** believe that the Liebenzell Mission holds four main distinctives," Ernst emphasized as he addressed a large missions conference in Germany. "Prayer is the first distinctive. Our founder, Rev. Heinrich Coerper, was poor, but he was a man of prayer. He prayed for the whole world, often hours each day. He lived by faith that the Lord would provide. And God certainly did, although most of the mission's growth has come since Rev. Coerper's death. We encourage our missionaries, above all, to be people of prayer.

"Faithfulness to God's Word is the second distinctive. Many people do not believe that God will conduct Himself as He has revealed in His Word. But He does. Our mission believes that God is the sovereign author of the Bible. Thus we are a mission that teaches the Bible as the literal Word of God and seeks to practice it as such.

"Faith is the third distinctive. Our eyes are on the Lord, not circumstances. Our main work is to believe God and seek Him always for everything. This leads to great testing when God seems not to be responding to a crisis or a need. It also leads to miraculous events in which God undertakes to perform the impossible.

"Sacrificial commitment to reach the unreached people in Germany and around the world is our fourth distinctive. I must say that we have people who have sacrificed comfort and family to take the gospel around the world. I know how sacrifice impacts the heart of another. I myself was influenced toward Christ by the sacrifice of a man in a prison camp during the war. His name was Robert. We were starving, given only one piece of bread and some corn each day. I saw men fight like animals over a crumb. Everyone was desperate. We thought of nothing but food and survival. One day Robert offered to give me half of his bread. I asked how he would be able to make such a sacrifice. He said he'd do it with the help of the Lord Jesus. That sacrifice impressed me to want to be like him. Likewise, I see many of our missionaries and supporters winning people by making great sacrifices in the name of the Lord."

The meeting ended and the crowd milled around. Suddenly, Ernst found himself looking into the broad chest of a large, elderly man. His neck appeared strong, his head balding. His rounded shoulders were thick with muscle. Ernst placed his hand into the man's massive hand, then tilted his head back to look up into his warm, penetrating eyes.

"Hello," said the man. "I deeply appreciate what you said tonight. I've been following you in the Liebenzell newsletters and praying for you for many years."

"Thank you very much. And what is your name?"

"Robert Vatter."

Time froze. Ernst's body shuddered and his breathy words stumbled over one another. "Robert Vatter from the prison camp?" He asked as he gazed at the man before him in a wide-eyed stare.

"Yes," Robert replied. His eyes were moist.

"Praise the Lord that I could see you again. I never knew what happened to you after you got me released from the truck at the Rhine. I remember how terrified I was not knowing if I could survive working in the coal mines in France. Only someone like you can understand the emptiness of facing possible death in a foreign land without your family ever knowing what happened. But, most of all, I want to thank you. You didn't just talk about your faith, you lived it. That was the first time Christianity had an influence upon my life—and the first time I ever thought that I wanted to become a Christian if I could be like you."

"I never imagined that," Robert replied humbly. "But I am most grateful to the Lord."

"Well, it's all true. Come, I want to introduce you to Sigrid, then we must sit down over coffee and talk for a few minutes."

Spotting his wife in the crowd, Ernst called, "Sigrid, please come here. This is Robert Vatter, the man from the prison camp that I told you about."

"Mr. Vatter . . ." Sigrid began as tears welled up in her eyes.

"Hello, Mrs. Vatter. It's nice to meet you."

"I want to thank you for the way you helped my husband."

Robert blushed. Ernst said, "Now we are going to get some coffee and talk."

"Yes, I'm sure the two of you have much to talk about," said Sigrid. "I will leave you alone."

The men went to a café and sat at a small round table on the outside patio. The aroma of coffee swirled in the air. Steam rose from their cups as Robert began, "Just think, Adolf Hitler sold his soul to the devil to gain the whole world and lost both his soul and the world. I have watched as you sold your soul to the Lord and gained both your soul and the world. Hitler was destroyed in flames, but you have since taken the fire of truth from the flaming mountain to every corner of the world."

Ernst stared beyond Robert and deep into the past. He spoke slowly, meaningfully. "And it all started with you giving me physical bread that led to the Bread of Life. I knew you had something that the other men in the camp lacked. I witnessed things there I never dreamed existed."

For an instant, the past revisited both men: sights, sounds, smells. Then Robert snapped them back to the present. "That place must have made a tremendous impression upon your young mind."

"Yes, it not only reduced everyone to an equal level, but it destroyed all confidence in man-made philosophies, such as that of the Third Reich. Perhaps that's what has deepened my conviction that the gospel is the only message worth preaching. But I could only have seen that through the sharp contrast between you and the other men. You presented true manhood with grace, dignity and strength amid inhumanity. That's what attracted me to the faith."

Robert looked down at the floor, then cleared his throat and said, "What Satan meant for evil God meant for good. I'm sure that the prison camp largely shaped your perception of the true value of real life."

"Yes, that's right. Many of the younger missionaries who have not suffered cling to things that perish. Some demand security, complain about small things and quit when times get tough. I can't blame them. They were raised that way by their families and schools, raised to think life owes them something. They find it hard to surrender their freedom in order to fulfill the purposes of God."

"I don't think, Ernst, anyone is fit to serve the Lord with power and authority until all of life has been stripped away and they learn what matters. You can't preach or teach it to them. It must come from experiencing the sufficiency of God alone. It often comes through some tragedy, like the death of a child. However it comes, it impacts them as the prison camp impacted us. Then they're fit for service, provided they respond properly by faith."

"That's true. I don't want anyone to go through what we faced, but everyone needs something to strip them to bare existence. Even Jesus learned obedience by what He suffered. Having endured the desert, Satan presented Him with three easy solutions for His suffering. It was only after refusing the temptations that He went to Galilee with power and authority."

There was a lull in the conversation as Robert sipped his coffee and pondered. Then, lowering his cup, he said, "Isn't it strange that one's perspective on everything is best shaped when one has nothing?"

"Yes," Ernst responded. "In the prison camp we lost our lives without choice and discovered raw humanity. In Christ we lose our lives by choice and discover pure sovereignty."

"What else have you learned over the years?" Robert asked.

"Through travel I have discovered that the only worldwide functioning society is the Church of Jesus Christ. No matter where you go, the people who have the kingdom of God within them share a universal relationship. They extend prayer, comfort, encouragement and help. There is clear evidence of a living God in His living Church. Certainly it has many shortcomings, but it is the only society that functions globally."

Robert listened, his cup raised in both hands with the rim resting on his chin. He said, "So in large measure the prayer of Christ for the oneness of His Body is being answered."

"Indeed. I feel at home anyplace in the world. And it's amazing how the Lord leads this global society to help one another. We have the thing that the world lacks—unity of heart around the cross of Christ."

"I want you to know, Ernst, how deeply I was drawn to pray for you while you were ill. I have read of the unusual ways God has answered prayer in your ministry. Tell me an unpublished story."

"It's amazing. Medical tests say that I should not be alive right now. But I'm here. Although, I must be careful about catching a cold or the flu, since they disturb other problems that could end my life. Even here, however, I've seen the Lord undertake. Once—it was shortly after Christmas—I caught a severe cold and had a high fever. The doctor came to my home and gave me an injection. Afterward he sat down and played a hymn on our piano. He said, 'The injection is for your body. This hymn is for your soul.' Then he left.

"Sigrid had to leave for the weekend to speak at a women's conference. She was afraid to leave, but I said, 'Please go. I won't die.'

"The fever never lifted throughout the weekend. The doctor came back, examined me and said, 'Mr. Vatter, you don't have enough iron in your blood. You must eat some dark meat or something to rebuild your iron, or I'll have to give you medication.'

"I said, 'OK, doctor, you go home and I'll look after that.'

"After he left I prayed, 'Lord, you know what is in the deep freeze in the cellar, but I can't go down there with this fever. Please undertake for me. Both my wife and the doctor are gone, but You are still here.' I kept talking to the Lord until late afternoon. Suddenly, the phone rang and a farmer who lived 100 kilometers away said, 'Brother, may I come over to visit you?'

"I said, 'You may come, but you cannot stay long. I'm very sick.'

"He arrived two hours later and sat by my bed. I asked point blank, 'Now, tell me why you have not come in over a month, but felt led to come today.'

"He took a metal container out of his travel bag and handed it to me saying, 'Yesterday I killed a pig and we had a feast. I made some blood sausages. I know you like them. I brought some for you.'

" 'Brother,' I said, 'I never thought about you, but have been praying for God to supply food for me.'

"He said, 'It was the Holy Spirit who told me to come and my wife who urged me to bring the sausage.' And all that time I had been lying there praying and believing that God would supply my needs. After he left I ate all of it.

"The next day the doctor came. I said, 'Doctor, forget it. There's no longer a problem. I have enough iron.' I was well in a couple of days. Robert, I've seen the Lord meet my needs like that many times. But more importantly, I've seen Him open doors for the gospel around the world in unimaginable ways. Nearly always it happens through this global society called the Church."

The evening grew late. The two comrades in faith rose and grasped hands, like two mighty warriors serving the same kingdom. They looked at each other without a word.

Brotherhood spoke loudly in the silence. Then Robert said, "I will continue to pray for you, Ernst."

"And I shall ever be indebted to you, Robert."

Thus, they parted, savoring their sacred encounter.

CHAPTER THIRTY-SIX

The Shock of Silence

The spring of 1993 confronted Ernst with a new challenge: He knew that within a year he would have to step down as the overseas director. Retirement: The calendar demanded it, but his spirit and body denied it. Twelve years in Japan and twenty-four years as overseas director felt like the starting block, not the finish line. *Is God bound to a calendar? Did men of the Bible know retirement? Does the Lord have more for me?* Those questions would have to wait until he handed the reins to the new director and passed into this unknown time of his life.

As usual, Ernst was poring over his Bible at the sun's early blaze. His eye fell upon Psalm 119:140, "Your promises have been thoroughly tested, and your servant loves them."

Indeed, Lord, he prayed, *You set the stage for me to see Your magnificent promises undergirded by Your faithful Word. You have delivered me, sustained me, protected me, blessed me, enabled me to persevere. . . .*

He wandered for a moment through the corridors of memory looking at the exhibits of fulfilled promises. Then he resumed: *I have held nothing back, but rather sought to trust You with all I had. You have been more than faithful, flooding me with things I didn't deserve: life, healing, family, friends, honor, accomplishments. Now, I choose to prove You in this phase of my life as*

*well. Surely Your power is not diminished by my age. Enable me
to help the new director get fully established.*

The first thing on Ernst's agenda when he entered his office that morning was to phone Detlef Krause, a missionary who had just returned to his post in Papua New Guinea.

"Good morning, Detlef. This is Ernst Vatter."

The two chatted for a few minutes, then Detlef asked, "Why have you called me today?"

"The time has come for me to retire from the position of overseas director. The board and I have discussed the matter and believe you are the man God would have to take my place. We would like you to come home immediately, work under my supervision for one year, then take over full time."

"I feel deeply honored to be considered for this position," Detlef replied, "but having just returned to this field I would not feel right leaving so quickly. May I request that I be given one more year to put everything in order before returning to Germany?"

"Yes, very good. We will make adjustments and expect you to return next spring."

That's the kind of maturity needed for the job, Ernst thought as he hung up the receiver. *Surely he's the right man.*

Ernst felt the year pass like sand through his fingers. He was startled when he flipped his calendar to April 1, 1994, and read: *Retirement celebration.* He had seen it in his peripheral vision, but now it was directly before his eyes. Detlef was still in Papua New Guinea when hundreds gathered on "fire mountain" for an entire day of praise to God and in honor of Ernst's forty-seven years of service. Missionaries, ministers, friends and representatives from other Christian organizations joined the entire staff and student body to spend the day in ceremony and celebration.

No one gave God more glory than Ernst as the roster of his accomplishments was revealed. No one knew better than he that it resulted from direct acts of God and not because of his natural strength or abilities. Still, he listened uncomfortably as the impressive list was read.

"Under Ernst's leadership the foreign outreach of Liebenzell Mission has expanded from five to twenty-two fields, and the mission force has grown from sixty to 220. Ernst replaced central control with work divisions and delegated responsibilities. He helped to foster the family atmosphere within the mission, guarding it to remain people-oriented. This philosophy webbed its way from the administration to the missionaries and on to the supporting churches and individuals.

"As a result of Ernst's work, five new buildings stand on 'fire mount,' including the beautiful retirement home for the Sisterhood. Biola University, in Los Angeles, California, granted him an honorary doctorate for his contribution to furthering the German Evangelical Mission world outreach. With Ernst's assistance, the mission festival for youth that is held each year at 'fire mountain' has grown from several hundred in attendance to over 6,000 in two gatherings. He also cofounded Help For Brethren, the relief organization that gives in excess of 1 million marks a year to assist churches and Bible schools around the world.

"For twenty years Ernst chaired the Association of Evangelical Missions in Germany and served as a member of the Lutheran Synod, covering the state of Wuerttemberg, for eighteen years. And finally, he was the president of the Missions Commission of the World Evangelical Fellowship for six years."

Ernst felt deeply honored and humbled by the speeches of the Bishop of the Lutheran Church of Wuerttemberg and other dignitaries, but found himself privately reminiscing his own story as he had lived it. He realized what the others did not know—that his decision at age two to live with his aunt had begun his path toward conversion. From there, the Lord had continued to direct that path, using both extraordinary events and people.

Glancing at Sigrid, who was listening intently to the speakers, Ernst thought, *This is the true heroine of the day. She has prayed me through to victory many times. Surely, she is the wife of noble character spoken of in Proverbs 31. My heart has been able to safely trust in her.*

Continuing to retreat into his own thoughts, he reminisced about how death had tried to escort him off the planet, but then had to surrender him to God's power, though it was permitted to keep a daily eye on him ever after. Ernst marveled over the two children whom the doctor said could never be born, and heard his doctor's strong warning, "Don't travel. It will kill you." But here he sat on this day thirty-five years and five continents of travels later.

He was jolted back to reality when the audience stood for the benediction. As the day ended, Ernst glanced to the top of "fire mountain" and prayed for God to empower his successor, Detlef Krause, who would now take the flame of the gospel to the world.

As the days went on, however, Ernst found himself reaching out to the Lord, not just on Detlef's behalf, but for himself as well. He realized that he needed strength to help him deal with a most difficult transition. Wisdom told him that he had to walk this valley alone, that to share it would not be good for the Liebenzell family. He drove home one day analyzing the wrestling within his heart. Suddenly it struck him: He was suffering the shock of silence. No longer was he hearing, "Mr. Vatter, what do you think about this?" or, "What shall we do about that?" or, "What are your plans now?" Instead he was hearing those questions posed to Detlef. He wasn't resentful; he simply felt the loss. That realization raised a whole new set of unexpected questions.

"Sigrid," he said that evening after dinner, "I have concerns that I never experienced before."

"What are they?"

"I find myself troubled that our phone rarely rings with people seeking my opinion or guidance. Then, when someone does ask for my advice, I must be careful to honor Detlef's position. I am fighting with the sense of uselessness that this brings, especially after so many years of being in the middle of everything."

"In the middle, nothing! You were at the head of it. Now you feel as if you're on the sideline."

"That's true. I have noticed a positive side to the silence, however. I am spending more time than ever with God in His Word, and I am finding wonderful truths. I also get to spend more time at home, since I don't have to travel as much. Being here with you has become the central interest of my heart."

Sigrid smiled. "That's very nice to hear. What is good is that the Lord protected us from growing apart during the years of travel. Now, in this time we can enjoy being together more often."

"There are other things bothering me now that I have time to think about them. Often I was invited to the homes of wealthy people. They expected me to rejoice over all they had acquired, but rarely did they give sacrificially to the gospel. It seems unfair to me that, as a servant of the gospel, I do not even have the funds to remodel this house to make it nice for you."

"Ernst, I know this house could use some fixing up, but even if it never happens, I'm happy. We may not have much of a house, but we have a wonderful home. And, above all, we have the things that really matter."

"I know that's true. Your spirit has always been a blessing to me. But I hope that I can do something for you some day. Also, I would like to be able to leave more to our children to help them in the ministries God has called them to."

"Ernst, you held nothing back from God, and I believe He will continue to hold nothing back from you. Already He has shown His heart toward you."

"How's that?"

"You have always loved fine cars, but you were not able to drive one, so as not to give the wrong impression to supporters. Now, in your retirement, the Lord directed people to provide you with your small BMW."

Ernst grinned, unable to deny the truth. He replied, "I feel as though the Lord has saved the best for last. Thank you, Sigrid. There is no way for me to adequately repay you for the wife you have been all these years. And now I get to enjoy you more."

"It's not over yet, Ernst. Through the years it has been in our weakest, most desperate times that we have seen the strong arm of the Lord. I believe that God is still going to use you in marvelous ways. I think we are in for some more surprises."

CHAPTER THIRTY-SEVEN

An Ending . . . and a New Beginning

"**G**ood morning, Detlef," greeted Ernst. "This is my final day as your advisor. To-morrow you're on your own."

"My, this day has come too quickly. I wonder if we could have lunch together. There are some questions I need to ask you," responded Detlef.

"Yes, indeed. Let's meet at noon."

The two men met punctually. It was the late spring of 1995. They sat outside at a café along the crooked road that carves its way through Liebenzell. Flowers cascaded from window boxes as bees darted from bloom to bloom. The place of meeting was Ernst's choice based upon his passion for ice cream.

"Ah, this coffee smells good," Ernst said, lifting his head to inhale the savory blend.

"Indeed it does," responded Detlef. "Ernst, throughout the past year I have asked you endless questions about the various countries where we serve. Today I want to ask you a different kind of question. Would you share with me some of the most important spiritual lessons you have learned?"

"I'd be happy to. There was a very difficult lesson I learned the day that Roy Hession spoke at Liebenzell. I was to translate for him that evening and had asked him what he would be speaking on. I wanted to see his notes in order to prepare. He said that he didn't know what his message would be. Later that day I went to his room to insist on seeing his notes. Still, he didn't know his subject. I got angry, I mean really angry. He said, 'Ernst, are you angry because you are concerned about God's glory, or are you angry because you're afraid you may look bad?'

"I had to admit to the latter. That's when I realized how deeply I was using God's service for my own glorification. That was a hard lesson. But I realized that to serve God wholeheartedly required deeper and deeper levels of death to self."

"Did you ever master dying to yourself?"

"No, of course not. That's a daily choice, and not always an easy one; in fact, it doesn't even get easier with age."

"What do you do when you feel that you have failed?"

"Confess. I've learned not to pamper my sin. I confess it to the Lord by name and trust Him to cleanse me as He promised in First John 1:9."

"Please," Detlef urged, "tell me another major lesson you have learned."

"Accept everything that comes into your life as from the hand of the Lord and be thankful for it. That was driven home to me in a powerful way by a Chinese evangelist named Pastor Wu. I believe he was eighty-three when I met him in the back room of a hotel somewhere in China. He had been arrested because he was an evangelist and was sentenced to fifteen years of imprisonment. He looked forward to his release but was overlooked when his sentence should have ended. Eight more years were lost in the prison, for a total of twenty-three years. I was amazed that he had no resentment toward the government and no bitterness toward the guards. Nor was he disturbed that God allowed all those years to be robbed from his life. His eyes were gentle and his voice peaceful and loving as he looked directly at me and said, 'Brother, I realized that the Lord thought it better for me to stay than to be released.'

"That was very moving to me. I believe that it will be through the commitment of men such as this that the gospel will one day spread across China. And you will probably be at the helm when it does. You may yet see the fulfillment of Hudson Taylor's vision and prayer."

"That would be a wonderful thing," Detlef responded. "My hope is to see missionaries advance the gospel into countries that are closed to it today."

"I'm pleased to hear that and will be praying to that end. It will be most important to keep the mission steadily on course with this purpose. While we send professional people to serve in the fields of business, education and medicine, it will be critical for them to understand that their skill is only the door opener for the gospel. I remember Pastor Wu saying, 'Never do anything else but preach the gospel. Social work is important, but not as much as preaching the gospel of the saving knowledge of the Lord Jesus Christ.' I determined that day to be more faithful than ever."

That evening, as Ernst drove home, he felt as though the pines were casting cold shadows across his soul. He tried to sing, but the songs felt empty. He tried prayer, but God seemed disinterested. At dinner Sigrid found him quiet, distant—trapped within himself.

"Ernst, what's wrong?"

"I had lunch with Detlef today."

"Is there a problem with him?"

"No, I couldn't be more pleased. He has vision and drive. He wants to get the gospel into the darkest regions of the world."

"So, then, what's the problem?"

"I've been trying to sort out my own feelings. Last year, when I officially retired, I felt the shock of silence that fell as people no longer sought my direction. But I still was called upon over the past year to advise Detlef. Now that's over too. The silence has become suffocating."

"This is certainly a new challenge to faith, isn't it?"

"That's a good way to put it. It's as though time raced ahead of my mind and body saying I must slow down, but nothing within me agrees. I still feel strong. My desire to serve is still intense. What do I do with all this energy?"

"Ernst," Sigrid commiserated, "you held nothing back from God when He sent you into the world. Don't hold anything back from Him now as He draws you closer to Himself. You were so busy that you had little time for deeper reflection. Now you have the time."

"You're right. I have experienced a whole new world of insight by spending more time in the Word and in prayer over the past year. But that has presented another problem. When I see these truths I want to share them, I feel like a dam filling up with no overflow."

"That may be true for now, but I believe God may open greater doors than ever for you to share those truths. If He can lift you from your deathbed as He did, then He can also raise you out of this silence. In fact, it's in the silence that the greater things to share will come. So you must use the silence well as God prepares you for further ministry—although, I think it's important to remember that God didn't save you to use you, but to love you. Your relationship with Him is more important than all the service in the world."

"Sigrid, you're wise. I have much to learn from you. Many times over the years I regretted having so little time to read, think and pray as a result of the steady flow of organizational decisions I had to make. I guess I have to adjust to this new experience. While activity has its endless noise, it's the silence that carries a rich symphony. But the adjustment isn't easy. The problem is that I'm retired but I'm not old. Old is a state of mind."

"Ernst, think of what God has done in your life so far. I don't think He has run out of creativity. We must trust Him for His purpose even now."

After dinner, Ernst went to his study to read and pray his way through Psalm 1:1-3: "Blessed is the man who does not walk in the counsel of the wicked or stand in the way of sinners or sit in the seat of mockers. But his delight is in the law of the LORD, and on his law he meditates day and night." *Lord*, he thought, *I must use this time You have given me to deepen my meditation.* Ernst continued reading: "He is like a tree planted by streams of water, which yields its fruit in season and whose leaf does not wither. Whatever he does prospers."

There is no age limit to this promise, he thought. Ernst finally sensed his heart quiet and noticed a new sound—the clock rhythmically ticking on the wall—as he drifted into peaceful sleep.

* * *

As with most of life, the ending of one phase is simply the beginning of a new one. Such was the case with Ernst's long career at the Liebenzell Mission. Though retired, he was pleased that he was still frequently asked to speak at conferences on behalf of the mission. The deeper truths he was learning in long hours of Bible study were put into sermons he would preach around the world. But each truth he preached he was required to practice as well, especially when confronting his gnawing concern about Annette's fate.

Anette had married Juergen Schuster, a Liebenzell missionary, and was working at his side during their second term in the land where Anette had spent the first five years of her life—Japan. She loved helping her husband in the work of the church, and untiringly distributed tracts and engaged herself in women's meetings. She spoke the Japanese language well and loved the people wholeheartedly.

Yet, in spite of the fulfillment she found in her ministry, Anette experienced a nagging grief: She and Juergen had no children. Anette felt like an outcast when the other missionary wives, happy young mothers, endlessly discussed their experiences in raising their cherished sons and daughters.

Year after year, Ernst had prayed that the Lord would bless Anette and Juergen with a child. Nearly everyone had given up hope, and Anette herself had resigned to what seemed to be God's will.

"Oh, God," Ernst sighed aloud, as he set the newsletter aside. "You know how my dear Anette longs to be a mother. We have been praying for twelve years. . . ."

The shrill ring of the telephone on his desk burst into his somber thoughts. Before Ernst could say "hello," an excited voice said, "Hi, Dad, how are you?"

"Well, I was just thinking about . . ."

But Anette, giddy with joy, didn't pause long enough for him to continue. "Dad, we're going to have a baby! Think of it! I wanted to tell you first, because I know that you have been praying for us for so long."

"Anette . . . really? Are you sure? You aren't joking, are you?"

"Well, of course I'm not joking! You're going to be a grandpa again. Juergen and I are so happy! Isn't it wonderful?"

And, indeed, it was a wonder that after so many years, God granted such a wonderful gift. Kimberly's birth on February 8, 1997, was another reminder to Ernst that he needed to trust God with each concern in every area of life—even when he was facing his own death.

CHAPTER THIRTY-EIGHT

Will the Warrior Rise Again?

"Good morning, Ernst," Sigrid cheerfully greeted as she drew back the curtains. "I'll start packing for you." All too soon the time of departure for the Pacific island of Koror, Palau had arrived and Ernst still could not lift his head from the pillow. Like an alarm, Sigrid's voice startled him back to the present—a present scantily clad with promise.

It was June of 1999. For three days Ernst had been virtually confined to bed, fully expecting he'd have to cancel the trip. Even in Ernst's retirement, Satan had continued harassing him with weakness each time he was departing to speak, generally on one of the fields he had helped to open to the gospel. This time, the weakness turned mysteriously worse. Ernst could do little more than stare at the ceiling—debilitated, motionless—retracing the footsteps of his past. His memories were like old friends arriving unexpectedly, communing with nostalgic delight.

Would this present weakness be the end of his ministry? Or would God once again raise him up to serve? Uncertain, he could only wait.

"Sigrid, I can't go to Palau. It's never been like this before. I still think we should call a doctor," Ernst protested.

His words fell to the floor, powerless, as Sigrid looked down into his eyes and declared, "You will go to Palau today. We have already put that before the Lord."

Resigned, he rested silently as Sigrid packed his suitcase with determination. He didn't dare mention that he was sure she'd be unpacking by day's end.

An hour passed. Ernst was surprised when he tried raising his head and discovered that it responded. "Hmph," he grunted. Next he raised his arm, then let it flop to the bed. He ventured to drop one leg over the side of the bed to see if he could sit up. His eyes radiated wonderment as his body rose to a sitting position. The next move was crucial. Could he stand and walk? Yes, he could!

Jubilant, he exclaimed, "Sigrid, look! . . . I'm up! . . . I'm walking!" He laughed and shuffled his feet in a comical dance. Strength rose from a source deep within.

She gave him an I-knew-it-would-happen-all-along look and placed the last folded shirt in his suitcase and then said, "OK, OK. Now you must hurry and get ready."

Ernst raced to the shower, thrilled to realize that God was not done using him. Throwing on travel clothes, he gave Sigrid a warm hug and a kiss, dashed out the door and was gone. She sighed and smiled.

Within hours Ernst was briskly striding through the Stuttgart Airport in full gait, cheerily waving at familiar faces behind ticket counters; people who had helped him on his countless flights over the years. Soon he was high in the sky soaring toward Palau. Opening his Bible, his eyes fell upon Psalm 84:7: "They go from strength to strength, till each appears before God in Zion."

He leaned back in his seat, looked out the window toward the shimmering horizon and thought, *That describes my life. All along God has been destroying my confidence in human strength in order to show me His. Indeed, I've been passing from strength to strength on my journey to Zion.* Then he prayed, *Lord, always before revealing Your strength You allowed the enemy to reduce mine, but never as these past days. I wonder what You plan to show of Your mighty power on this trip.* Long hours later Ernst arrived on Palau, strong and fit to preach at the conference.

While sitting at lunch one day, Ernst found himself surrounded by a group from the conference, responding to their requests to tell some of his life's stories. Two hours later every person at the table sat spellbound.

"Your story needs to be told in a book," said one of the co-speakers.

"Do you really think so?" asked Ernst.

"Absolutely. Your story is loaded with insights and encouragement for people of every age. Your life is a picture of perseverance."

Ernst's eyes momentarily stared into the distance as he wondered if this was the reason for the severe attack just prior to leaving for this trip. *Is God raising up a new ministry? Is it possible that the God who delivered me from death, sustained me in life and opened impossible doors intends to demonstrate His power to reinvent retirement, to use me as an exhibit that no one's story ever ends until he is called home?*

Returning to the conversation, Ernst commented, "It would be wonderful if God wants a book written. I can't imagine that happening, but if it did, I would like to see people learn three things from my story. The first is hope: hope in God and His promises. Second is faith to handle life in God's way. Third is prayer. An old German saying states, 'Make prayer out of everything.' While prayer moves the hand of God, it also enlarges the heart of man."

Ernst then turned to the passion of his heart: concern for the state of the Church worldwide. "Recently I heard on the radio that there are 5 million churches, 25,000 denominations, 6 million pastors and 1.9 billion Christians. In light of this, one would expect the Church's impact upon the world to be greater."

"What's hindering us?" someone asked.

"Materialism for one. I think it's more dangerous than communism ever was. It lures people into spiritual laziness, a false sense of security. This leads to another: options eroding obligations and convenience killing commitment. People skip from church to church and do not commit themselves to obligations in any one place. That dissipates effectiveness. Third is the shift from doctrinal content to personal experience. Many run from diligent Bible study and race toward questionable experiences. Too many pastors are playing into the hands of experiences, hoping to draw crowds. When the church is not sound in doctrine, it cannot be sound in soul.

"The fallout is dire. Young people are not committing themselves to the task of world evangelism as before. My successor Detlef Krause told me that during my years as overseas director, the missionary count went from sixty to 220. In the past eight years, however, it has only increased by ten new missionaries."

"Perhaps," someone interjected, "God intends to use your story to encourage many to reverse that. Would it not be a tremendous thing to see a whole new wave of people inspired to believe God and unreservedly give themselves to taking the gospel to the world?"

Ernst nodded, paused from drinking his mineral water and said, "That would really be something. Nothing would give me greater joy or fulfillment." His eyes had a fresh sparkle of hope.

One of the members of the group seized this rare opportunity to question the man who had walked through so many unusual experiences with God. "If you could address the whole Church worldwide, what would you say?"

"Have no god but God: not a spouse, not a child, not a desire. Hold nothing back from God and He won't hold one good thing back from you. That's His promise. I must say that God is true and faithful to His Word. His love will never fail. If we tend to His commands, He'll tend to our concerns."

"If you could address every pastor and teacher in the world at one time, what would you say?"

"The cross is our central message. You can go deeper in the cross, but you can never go higher or further. We must stop cluttering the cross. If we preached the cross every Sunday for a lifetime, we would never exhaust the ways it delivers us from ourselves, directs us beyond ourselves and draws us to the throne of God. We must return to the cross or we have no worthy message for the world."

"If you knew that this was your last day on earth, and television cameras were waiting to take your final words to the entire world, what would you say?"

"I would shed tears as I said good-bye to my wife and children. I would say it's not easy to part from those you love. But it's a wonderful thing, even in such a painful time, to know that one will eventually be with his loved ones and the Lord Jesus forever. My whole life has been lived with the assurance that the Lord has prepared a place for me to go with my loved ones after this life is over. My challenge is this: Do you have a goal to go to heaven when you die? Think about that. If that's your desire, there is a living God who offers you the solution in Jesus Christ. He is the way. Believe in Him.

"Then I would tell them a story: When I was in Japan I knew a judge who became a pastor. Surprised, I asked him how that happened, since his family was not interested in Christ. He said, 'My mother called me to my dying sister's bedside. My sister was already unconscious but suddenly opened her eyes and, with tears running down her cheeks, asked, "Mom, what comes now?" My mother, who is highly educated said, "I don't know, my daughter, I don't know." Those were the last words spoken to my sister as she passed into eternity. After the funeral my mother came to me and said, "Son, I would like to get the answer to my daughter's last question." In our search we discovered that only Jesus Christ, who Himself was raised from the dead, can wash away our sins and grant us resurrection into heaven. Out of gratefulness to the Lord I turned from law to become a pastor.'

"So you see, nothing matters so much as preparing to pass from this life. My own sister's daughter, Esther, had a stroke at the young age of twenty-three. My sister asked me to rush to the hospital, which I did. But my niece died before I arrived. My sister told me that she opened her eyes before being rushed into the operating room and said, 'Mom, don't be afraid. Jesus goes with me.' Then Esther looked at her brother and said, 'Bernd, believe in Jesus! The only help you'll ever get in life is when you turn your life over to Jesus.' Those were her last words. Two years later Bernd told me, 'Uncle, I couldn't forget Esther's final words. I gave my heart to the Lord. I'm a child of God.'

"Soon everyone will pass through death. Have you turned to the only One who can save you from the grave? That's what I would say to the world."

The conference ended and Ernst returned to Germany. Opening the door to his home, he was slapped in the face by the large, wet tongue of Struppi—a black and white sheepdog with a touch of German shepherd blood. The suitcase sat by the door while Ernst laughingly wrestled with his pet. "Ah, Struppi, I waited so many years since Rico to have you. You always give me a hero's welcome, whether I come home in the middle of the day or night. But I don't think I'll try to ride you, since I'm too big and you're too small." Sigrid stood in the doorway smiling while Ernst and Struppi burned off some energy.

After an embrace Sigrid asked, "Well, how did the conference go?"

"The conference went well, but something strange happened. It was suggested that a book be written about my life."

"That's great! I think you have an incredible story to be told. God indeed had something unique in mind for the devil to attack you with such severity before you left for Palau. Obviously God is not through with you yet."

CHAPTER THIRTY-NINE

No Sunset in Sight

"Ah, Ernst, look. Here's an invitation for you to speak at the missionary conference in Japan next year. What a wonderful opportunity this would be for us to return to our beloved Japan."

"Yes, yes, I think we should go."

In July of 2000, Sigrid packed for their six-week trip to Japan. There were many people and places to see, but something special was on both of their minds. They slated the third week of August to tour Tokyo by train, particularly to see if *their* bench was still at the Todai Station. On the train ride into Tokyo, they entertained themselves by recalling many events.

"Ernst, I hope the 'demon' never returned to the church home."

"Yes, it was the mighty kitten who drove the marten away."

"And do you remember the time . . ." Sigrid teased, "you were taking the shortcut through the farmer's backyard and fell through the rotten timbers and into his cesspool!"

Both roared with laughter. Ernst caught his breath and said, "Ah, yes, we have so many crazy, wonderful memories. By the way, speaking of memories, we must switch here to get to the Todai Station. I hope our bench is still there."

The whistle screamed and the wheels screeched as the train slowed at Todai. Ernst and Sigrid drew quiet. Nearly half a century had come and gone since the days of meeting on *their* bench. Life had been a rich blend: the miraculous and the mundane, the dreams and the disappointments, the triumphs and the troubles—all salted with laughter and tears. People bumped and scrambled as they crisscrossed getting on and off the train, oblivious to the divine story in their presence.

Ernst and Sigrid stretched to look . . . only to realize that the bench was gone.

"Ah, so, Sigrid, it's gone. But it's no longer needed. We may have built our dreams sitting on that little bench, but we built our lives standing on the promises of God."

The train slowly pulled away from the station. Ernst and Sigrid felt no loss. They had gone from that small garden of romance to conquer life through the power of God. Now they enjoyed a mature love weathered by storms, strengthened by commitment, mellowed by age. They had faced the tough choices by remaining steadfast to God's Word, choosing conviction over compromise. And it worked! God had proven Himself true.

But faith is never without new kinks to challenge its confidence in God. Both Ernst and Sigrid were coughing as they boarded for home on August 29. For Sigrid a cold was just a cold, but not so for Ernst. By the time they arrived home, he was sinking fast. He had only seven days before his next scheduled departure—a conference in Zambia, a country dead center on the African continent, south of the equator.

By September 4—the day before Ernst's trip—he feared the worst. Pain shot like lightning through his chest each time he coughed. "Sigrid, I don't think I can go tomorrow."

"Nonsense! You will go. The devil will not get the victory."

Ernst groaned, thinking it best not to argue with the queen of tenacity.

The next morning, Sigrid packed Ernst's suitcase while he went to the doctor. He hoped that medical reinforcement would convince Sigrid that this time he should stay home. Tired of travel, he longed to feel the end to summer's heat and, for once, see the turning of the leaves in Germany. His state of malaise provoked nostalgic craving, the desire to coddle his cold in the comfort of home with Sigrid. Should he depart that afternoon, he'd be flying to a land that could prove hostile to his health, even in the best of times.

"Doctor Pfeifer, I'm to depart for Zambia this afternoon. Should I cancel my trip?" His tone was more of a plea than a question.

Following a thorough examination, the doctor presented the bad news. "It's just your muscles. You have coughed so hard and so much that you have strained the muscles in your chest. You'll be happy to know that there's no reason for you not to go to Zambia today."

Less than overjoyed, Ernst returned home to gather his bags. Sigrid stood in the doorway wearing a victorious smile as he lugged himself and his bags to the car. That evening he departed Frankfurt for London. He sat hunched over and coughing at Heathrow Airport as he awaited his next flight. He reasoned to himself, *With God leading from the front and Sigrid pushing from behind, I guess*

I'll survive. Both his body and emotions grumbled and argued otherwise.

That night he boarded his twelve-hour flight. The plane
headed south, crossed the equator, then circled to land in
Ndola, Zambia.

Upon deplaning, Ernst found himself smack dab in the
middle of Africa's southern hemisphere, near the southern
border of Zaire. He had left in Germany's early autumn and
arrived in Zambia's early spring, all in the same twenty-four
hour period. The rainy season had ended and the sky was a
beautiful cloudless blue.

He mustered the strength to stumble toward a waiting
car. "It's wonderful to have you here, Dr. Vatter. Thank
you for coming," greeted the driver.

"I'm happy to be here," Ernst replied, which being inter-
preted meant, "Get me to a bed." But even in Zambia people
knew of his condition and had been praying. He had two
days to rally enough strength to address the gathering of
three Baptist groups. He knew that the return of his health
was a hopeless prospect unless God answered prayer.

They arrived at the former mission compound at
Mpongwe which sat at the edge of the Copper Belt. The
compound was comprised of a hospital, church and mission
headquarters on the edge of 2,500 acres of mission-owned
farmland. Rent was paid to the hospital by a vegetable farmer
who worked the land. A few of the acres, however, were des-
ignated for the 4,000 people soon to swarm upon the compound for the conference.

The next day Ernst watched, unbelieving, as people began
to arrive from 400 miles to the north and from 100 miles to
the east and west. At first it was a trickle . . . then a stream . . .
then a flood of humanity. They came in old trucks, dilapi-

dated cars and on rusty bikes. Some even traveled by foot in thin-soled shoes. The flat acres were divided with straw barricades: Women would sleep here, men would sleep there, eating would take place over here and bathroom facilities were over there. Instinct created invisible paths to each location. Within hours, the barren reddish-brown field was carpeted with colorful, breathing life.

The sight invigorated Ernst's soul. Time marched forward, but his sickness dragged its feet. Wondering how effective he could be while feeling as limp as a dishrag, he rose to bring his first of four messages. Before him sat a city block of people, filled with expectation to "hear a word from God."

Ernst was amazed at the solemn order that prevailed. Many sat in the shade of trees that were strung together with long strands of speaker cords. Speaker boxes hung from branches, giving new meaning to trees lifting up the praises of God. The women wore large, light sari-like dresses that draped from their heads and hung freely to the ground, billowing like tents in the breeze. The men dressed in western-style shirts, trousers, sandals, jackets and sweaters. The throng sang without instruments, sending a tsunami of sound from earth to heaven. All shared two things in common—piety and poverty—yet their lifeless economy could not steal the life in their souls.

When Ernst opened his mouth, he found that he had to speak softly, otherwise he'd fly into a coughing fit. But a divine provision was in place. Was it an instant miracle of strength? No. It was the strength of his translator, Rev. L. Popo. While Ernst sounded like a whispering brook, Popo sounded like a roaring waterfall, projecting the passion and points that Ernst intended.

It was at the close of Ernst's third message that he witnessed the power of commitment over poverty. As he concluded, his statements fired Popo, who used them to ignite
a bonfire amid the crowd.

"Our mission to the world results from who and what we
are in Christ Jesus. Nobody can do our mission for us—not
angels, not anyone else. Only Christians can fulfill the great
commission. God has given it to us alone.

"Our prayers are too self-centered. Let's reduce prayers for
ourselves by fifty percent and use the rest to pray for lost
souls and the needs of our brothers and sisters in Christ.

"We live as though we're not convinced lost people will
go to hell. General William Booth, founder of the Salvation Army once said, 'If it would be possible, I would send
our mission candidates into hell for twenty-four hours so
that they would realize what it means to be lost and to
know how precious a soul is.'

"Some Christians live as though they are on a conveyor
belt taking them automatically to heaven, without any ob-
ligation on their part. While it's true that salvation is free,
it isn't cheap. Christ gave His life for us. Should we not
give ours for Him? We are called to labor, serve and love.
We are His body: His eyes, mouth, hands, feet. We are His
witness to the world. You are the only Bible most people
will ever read.

"There are many young pioneer church workers taking
what you believe to the world. Their sacrifice must not ex-
ceed ours. You must love and support them in every way possible."

Ernst sat down, thankful he had been able to present
the message. But he was about to witness a spectacle rare
to wealthy cultures: a truly sacrificial response. Rev. Popo

returned to the microphone to say, "We must act upon this message now. There is a space here in front of the platform. I'm not asking you to give money. But give what you can. We will send your gifts to our missionaries. What we can't send, we'll sell and distribute the money to them."

Ernst was stunned. He was accustomed to affluent audiences giving compliments—not commitments—in response to his straight talk. Popo called for immediate action. Ernst wondered what they could give. They were poor—dirt poor. Slowly, however, streams of people poured to the front, stacking gifts: ties, jackets, blankets, shoes, scarves, handkerchiefs, stockings, slippers, vests, shirts. . . . No one had come prepared to give, but all gave something nonetheless. Some placed on the pile pieces of paper with written promises of what they would give when they returned home.

It was far more than a pile of stuff, it was a statement of love. Items flowed out of poverty as though it were a horn of plenty. The pile blossomed and grew until the flower of sacrificial love was almost nine feet long, six feet wide and four feet high. Ernst slipped off his tie—a keepsake he had just bought in Japan—and laid it on the sacred altar.

Flying home the next day, he thought about life's brutal incongruities. *For these people, poverty was no barrier to giving, while for others, prosperity barricades generosity. Why is it that the more people have, the more they fear not having? Why do the poor give excessively, while the prosperous give excuses? How dare we think that lip service can replace washing feet! Do we truly think God is blind to our greed?*

Back at home, Sigrid unpacked his suitcase while he unburdened his soul. "Sigrid, how can it be that people give more out of poverty than prosperity? Do we think the widow's mite is just a cute story? Why can't we see it as a call to be Christlike in our giving?"

"I fear that many Christians are sacrificing eternal rewards for a brief pleasure today," Sigrid replied.

"There are people, like my aunt who lived in the castle, who seek to manipulate with money. Others try to impress with money. Still others imagine power and protection coming from money. What troubles me is that these are people who say they love God."

"It's certainly true, Ernst, that one cannot serve both God and money. Just imagine what could happen through the church and missionary outreaches if *all* Christians sacrificed for the sake of the gospel. God paid with His Son's life, and we give Him merely a Sunday tip."

"If God's people obeyed, every ear in the world could hear the gospel. But few are willing to live threadbare lives in order to translate the Scriptures, plant radio and television stations, work in hot, dusty hospitals and teach in ill-equipped Bible schools to take God's only salvation to the world."

"Ernst, if it disturbs us, how much more must it break the heart of God?"

"Sigrid, I've decided that I'm going to spend all day tomorrow in prayer."

Rising before dawn, Ernst climbed the steps with a steady gaze and determined gait, his Bible sheathed under his arm like a sword. He felt the same flame burning in his soul that had been ignited many years earlier on the night he met God in the village of Goenningen. The battles through the years left him with granite-like faith—powerful! His experience with the Zambian people filled him with broken boldness: broken in heart, bold in spirit.

Clicking on the tiny desk lamp, he opened his Bible to the book of Joshua and sat down. The early sun split the night open to illuminate the theater where Ernst prepared to approach his God. The light sloped across the seventh chapter of Joshua. Ernst's reading was interspersed with prayer:

Lord, I'm impressed by the story of Caleb. When he was forty, Moses sent him to spy out the Promised Land. His associates saw the giants in the land and warned Moses and the people not to enter. The people's hearts melted with fear. But Caleb was different. He followed You wholeheartedly, insisting that they take the land. Instead, Israel dishonored You with unbelief and lost their lives in the wilderness.

Caleb was eighty-five when he asked to conquer the same mountain where the giants lived who had intimidated Israel forty-five years earlier. Age didn't stop him from attempting the impossible. He brought down the very people who had brought down Israel.

Now, my Father, here is my request. While I do not feel that I served You perfectly, I served You wholeheartedly. You closed the door on Hudson Taylor's dream of China but opened the door for a global vision. You answered Sister Lina Stahl's prayer to make this mountain like a volcano spewing the gospel around the world.

Today, Detlef desires to see many missionaries penetrate the darkest countries on earth with the gospel. But people are neither giving nor going as they should. Father, I'm asking to bring down the giants of prosperity who have enslaved Your people. I'm asking You to raise up hundreds, supported by the sacrificial gifts of thousands more, to take your precious salvation to the world.

Ernst began to pray out loud. With fevered passion, he got up and paced, gesticulating before the Lord. "It is Your will that none should perish, but that all should come to repentance. Satan did nothing to deserve the right to lost people. Your Son came to destroy the works of the devil. It was Your Son who gained all authority by His obedience on the cross. It was Your Son who paid the ultimate price for the sin of the world.

"In light of this, I'm calling upon You to grant the great work of Your mighty Spirit for Your honor and glory, for the fulfillment of Your purposes. As Caleb asked for the mountain of the giants, so I am asking You to send the flames of the gospel from this mountain to the darkest corners of the world, to gather a harvest worthy of Your holy name."

As the day began to dim, Ernst closed his Bible and descended the small stairway for dinner. "How was your day?" asked Sigrid as they ate.

"I met Caleb!"

"Oh?"

"Even at age eighty-five, Caleb still sought victories for the glory of God. Well, I'm only seventy-one! So as long as the Lord allows, I too will continue to seek victory for His glory. I will not give up until God has raised up an entire force of missionaries who will hold nothing back from Him in order to take the gospel to the world."

After dinner Ernst walked into the living room and sat down on a soft chair. He crossed one leg over the other, leaned his left elbow on the arm of the chair and rested his chin on his fist. His forefinger wrinkled his cheek as it pointed toward his temple—a portrait of deep contemplation. Struppi flopped down at his feet as though to consult with him.

Nearby sat Sigrid, twisting yarn around a needle. As the ball of yarn unraveled slowly on the floor, an emerging sweater dropped to her lap. Looking up when Ernst sighed deeply, she gazed long at the man with whom she had forged through life. His greying hair still swept dashingly back. A deep groove etched each side of his face. With the glow of the evening sun on his tanned skin, he looked like a stately bronze statue. She smiled as she noticed the same look in his eyes that she had seen for years—impassioned! determined!—and she liked what she saw.

"Ernst, what's the biggest goal in your life now?" she asked in a soft tone.

"Heaven. I know that I have much to do yet in this life, but the silence has taught me more than ever to set my mind on things above. I wish that this perspective had been stronger in me in my younger years.

"While above all else I enjoy sitting here with you, my dear Sigrid, I will travel and speak as long as the Lord enables me to persevere."

Ernst and Sigrid still live in Calw, Germany. Ernst continues to speak at churches, Bible and missionary conferences, as well as leadership training sessions for ministers and missionaries. Strongly preferring to travel with Sigrid, he continues to live each day as an enigma to medical science, and an affirmation that God fulfills His purposes in the lives of those who trust in Him.

Norman Vatter and his wife Conny live in Moosach, near Muenchen. They are the parents of six living children: twenty-year-old Cathrin, eighteen-year-old Mirijam, fifteen-year-old Anika, thirteen-year-old Jachin, eight-year-old Samuel and seventeen-year-old Michael, their foster son. Norman is employed by German Transalpine Oil Pipeline System in Muenchen. He and his wife are strong supporters of the Liebenzell Mission on behalf of his sisters and are involved in starting a new church in their village.

Iris Vatter is a student at the Columbia International University in Columbia, South Carolina. She is working on a Master of Divinity degree in missions in order to return to Burundi, Africa to assist in establishing a Bible school.

Anette and her husband Juergen Schuster live in Deerfield, Illinois, where Juergen is working on a Ph.D. in intercultural studies at Trinity Seminary. Their desire is to return to Bad Liebenzell in Germany where he will teach at the theological seminary of Liebenzell Mission. Their daughter Kimberly is four years old.

Evelyne is now Mrs. Markus Breuninger. She and her husband serve in Botswana, Africa, where Markus is a missionary pilot. They have three young children: four-year-old Elisabeth, three-year-old Johannes and one-year-old Daniel.

The Liebenzell Mission is a faith ministry supported by both fellowship groups and individuals. A seminary continues to train students at the main headquarters in Bad Liebenzell, Germany. Also, they continue to send missionaries around the world, with a new emphasis on Islamic countries currently closed to the gospel. The mission prints a bi-monthly publication, which can be subscribed to at no cost.

Missions Headquarters in Germany:
Liebenzeller Mission - ASZ
Postfach 1240
75375 Bad Liebenzell
Germany
Phone: (07052) 17-139

Missions Headquarters in the U.S.:
Liebenzell Mission USA
P.O. Box 66
Schooley's Mountain, NJ 07870
USA

Missions Headquarters in Canada:
Liebenzell Mission Canada
R.R. #1
Moffat, ON L0P 1J0
Canada